This book will be a tremendous help for those who want to reach their full potential and become great leaders. Dr. Gorveatte has masterfully interpreted some of John Wesley's eighteenth-century insights and leadership skills.

—L. D. BUCKINGHAM, CEO Buckingham Leadership Institute

Lead Like Wesley brings to light a valuable understanding of ministry leadership from two ministry leaders whose experience and understanding I value so much: John Wesley and Mark Gorveatte. You likely have heard of Wesley who changed the world in the 1700s. But you also need to hear from a contemporary mover and shaker—Mark Gorvette. Mark makes things happen. We need more like him!

—JIM GARLOW, lead pastor, Skyline Wesleyan Church, La Mesa, CA

Lead Like Wesley is easily one of the most outstanding books on helping leaders to be more effective. The subject matter is challenging, convicting, and consistent with scriptural principles. Gorveatte balances information with instruction, insight with inspiration, and intensity with investigation. This book reveals not only the standards leaders are called to know and do, but also challenges us to pursue them.

—ANTHONY M. GRAHAM, senior pastor, New Hope Family Worship Center, Brooklyn, NY

Gorveatte has masterfully culled powerful truths of ministry leadership from one of the great ministry geniuses in history and connected them to our church and community realities today. Learn to lead from the well-earned wisdom of Wesley.

—BENJI KELLEY, founding senior pastor, new**hope** Church, Durham, NC

Lead Like Wesley, is a must-read for any leader regardless of theological position. I learned a little more about Wesley and a whole lot more about leadership.

—KEITH LOY, lead pastor, Celebrate Community Church, Sioux Falls, SD

The world has been waiting for this book! How did Wesley lead such a movement? What principles guided him? How could he work with every level of society and see transformation take place? Mark Gorveatte has captured the heart of Wesley's leadership life and principles and makes a compelling case for character-based leadership.

—JO ANNE LYON, general superintendent, The Wesleyan Church

Mark Gorveatte's *Lead Like Wesley* delivers even more than it promises. The book is organized around John Wesley's twelve practical "Rules of a Helper" for lay church leaders. Not only does Gorveatte thoughtfully expand on each of these rules, but he also sets this eighteenth-century guidance in the context of today's leadership experts. This book offers a practical, substantial, and creative approach to preparing for the privileged challenge of church leadership.

—SHIRLEY A. MULLEN, president, Houghton College

Mark Gorveatte's knowledge of John Wesley is unsurpassed, and he does an exceptional job applying the leadership style of our movement's founder to the challenges we all face today. This is an excellent book written by an excellent communicator.

—EVERETT PIPER, president, Oklahoma Wesleyan University

Mark Gorveatte brings the wisdom of John Wesley into our current understanding of leadership and challenges us to rediscover the genius of the Wesleyan model that lies at the very core of our movement.

—KIMBERLY D. REISMAN, executive director, World Methodist Evangelism

LEAD LIKE
WESLEY

HELP FOR TODAY'S MINISTRY SERVANTS

Mark L. Gorveatte

wesleyan
PUBLISHING HOUSE
wphstore.com

Copyright © 2016 by Mark L. Gorveatte
Published by Wesleyan Publishing House
Indianapolis, Indiana 46250
Printed in the United States of America
ISBN: 978-1-63257-125-0
ISBN (e-book): 978-1-63257-126-7

Library of Congress Cataloging-in-Publication Data

Names: Gorveatte, Mark, author.
Title: Lead like Wesley : help for today's ministry servants / Mark Gorveatte.
Description: Indianapolis : Wesleyan Publishing House, 2016. | Includes
   bibliographical references.
Identifiers: LCCN 2016001656 | ISBN 9781632571250 (pbk.)
Subjects: LCSH: Christian leadership. | Wesley, John, 1703-1791.
Classification: LCC BX8349.L43 G67 2016 | DDC 253--dc23 LC record available
   at http://lccn.loc.gov/2016001656

To Dr. Kenneth and Anne Gorveatte (Dad and Mom). Thank you for not just preaching the gospel but living it. I love you.

CONTENTS

For additional free resources,
visit wphresources.com/leadlikewesley.

ACKNOWLEDGEMENTS

Like the turtle sitting on a fence post, you can be sure I did not get here alone. Acknowledgements is that brief section at the beginning of a book where a writer has the opportunity to affirm a few people who can be named in the available space and to offend the many who deserve to be in this space but are not. You will soon know which category you are in.

Thank you to Sherry, the love of my life. Thank you for believing in me and sacrificing so much in our journey together.

Thank you to Bob and Dot. Thank you for being my favorite in-laws and for sharing Sherry with me.

Thank you to John, Josiah, Joel, and Jordan. Having great children like you makes it harder to fail at parenting.

Thank you to Ruth, Beth, and Joel. I am glad to be part of a family that has become friends.

Thank you to Damian and Anne, Greg and Shelly, Wes and Claudia, Scott and Elizabeth, Paul and Susan, Chad and Julie, Greg and Becky, Chris and Mary, Ward and Joetta, and too many more to name here. We have dreamed and laughed and cried together, believing the best is yet to come.

Thank you to Jim, Debbie, Barbie, Laurel, and Debra. I could not ask for better ministry partners. Thank you for the successes we celebrated due, in large part, to your diligent work that was so often behind the scenes.

Thank you to Jo Anne Lyon, Ed Stetzer, Keith Loy, Mark Wilson, David Drury, Brent Dongell, and Richard Waugh. Thank you for encouraging me to go after this project and offering valuable input. Your commitment to writing inspired me.

Thank you to Laurel Buckingham, H. C. Wilson, Mick Veach, David Smith, Ivan Graham, and Wayne Schmidt. Thank you for making me better through the gift of "iron sharpening iron."

Thank you to Rachael Stevenson and Craig Bubeck for your gifts in patiently coaching a rookie writer.

Thank you to Howard Snyder and Kevin Watson. I am grateful for your scholarly advice. You spurred me to investigate the relevance of applying John Wesley's leadership principles today.

Most of all, I am indebted to Jesus Christ, my risen Lord and coming King who has "saved us and called us to live a holy life— not because of anything we have done but because of his own purpose and grace" (2 Tim. 1:9).

INTRODUCTION
JOHN WESLEY: LEADERSHIP EXPERT

Lead Like Wesley was written for leaders like you, serving in the church. This book was penned for people who volunteer to lead teams and small groups, serve on boards, and teach Sunday school classes, not just for those who serve as pastors.

The Hartford Institute estimates that there are 350,000 religious congregations in America.[1] If we conservatively estimate ten leaders per church, that means more than three million leaders like you serve their local church. You are not alone. And you are not crazy for investing your time and energy in the church. Every other human institution will perish in time, but Christ's church will endure. This book was written for you, with respect and appreciation, because you invest your leadership in the only cause that counts for eternity.

I kept two basic assumptions about you in mind as I wrote.

First, I assume that you have had a personal experience of the grace of God through faith in Jesus Christ as your Lord and Savior. If you have not yet crossed that line of faith, there are still helpful principles in this study. However, to lead like John Wesley, you must tap into the power source that he relied on—an active relationship with God through Jesus Christ.

Second, I anticipate that you have some appreciation for John Wesley's adventurous life and effective ministry. You do not need to be a Methodist historian to learn from his "Rules of a Helper." However, the more you know about their context and the challenges Wesley faced, the more you will appreciate the genius of his leadership.

WESLEY'S LEADERSHIP ENDURES

John Wesley (1704–1791) was a remarkable individual. A popularity poll conducted by the British Broadcasting Corporation in 2002 placed him fiftieth among the one hundred most influential Britons of all time.[2] Wesley ranked above such notable figures as King Arthur and Florence Nightingale but far behind Princess Diana and John Lennon. It could be debated that this ranking was more of a commentary on those surveyed than on Wesley's real and lasting impact. Nevertheless, it reveals one measure of the timeless and enduring nature of his influence.

Three hundred years ago, when there was no digital communication and the fastest means of travel was still horseback, John Wesley and his Methodist circuit riders blazed a trail of revival across England at a pivotal time in history. While the Methodists preached the good news of full salvation freely offered by God's grace, France was embroiled in a bloody revolution. The spiritual reformation led by Wesley and the Methodists paved the way for dramatic societal transformation in the British Isles.

Most researchers agree that Wesley traveled approximately 250,000 miles in his ministry, mostly on horseback, and preached more than 40,000 times. He wrote, edited, or translated at least 200 volumes. These included sermons, hymns, commentaries, text-books, and political tracts.[3]

His guide to health and home remedies, "The Primitive Physick," went through thirty-six editions, sold more copies than any of his other books, and was still being published in the 1880s.[4] The income from book sales during his lifetime, when adjusted for inflation, exceeded four million British pounds, or nearly six million US dollars. And Wesley gave nearly all of it away, choosing to live on the same salary as other leaders in the Methodist movement.

Wesley was more than a prolific speaker and writer. He launched schools, orphanages, microcredit loans for entrepreneurs, health clinics, and the first free pharmacy in England. He was equally at ease whether in the company of common people or the king of England. One of his great joys was being the beloved uncle to a host of nieces and nephews. When he died, more than 135,000 people were active members in the Methodist societies, and nearly one million people had been spiritually awakened by the Methodists' faithful proclamation of the gospel.

Today, more than seventy-five million people around the world belong to the various denominational streams that flowed from the Methodist movement Wesley faithfully led for more than fifty years.

Wesley was a leader. He accepted leadership as a trust given to him by others, a trust for which he would ultimately account to God. The Holy Club at Oxford was formed when his brother Charles and two other students asked the young professor to provide leadership to their spiritual pilgrimage.

Although George Whitefield, his beloved friend and sometime rival, had already preached to large crowds in the fields of Kingswood, it was Wesley who determined to preserve the fruits of their labor.

He did this by mentoring the newest converts in small groups. Soon after, Wesley laid the cornerstone for what would become Kingswood College, the first educational institution for the Methodist movement.

WESLEY WAS A LEADER OF LEADERS

One of the clearest evidences of Wesley's leadership ability was his capacity to recruit, develop, and deploy hundreds of Methodist laypeople as class leaders, stewards, and managers of their properties and collective enterprises. With more than a hundred thousand Methodists gathering in weekly classes and averaging a one-to-ten ratio of leaders to members, it is possible that there were as many as ten thousand people serving in leadership at this primary level. John Lenton, a Methodist historian, has identified at least 802 lay and ordained leaders who served under John Wesley's oversight from the early days of the movement in 1743 until his death in 1791. There were 541 active leaders under Wesley's direction at the time of his passing.[5]

That is a complex organization even by today's standards. How did Wesley manage so many volunteers? How was Methodist leadership structured to sustain the movement? Wesley did not leave a detailed operations and policy manual. He did not implement rigid rules that stifled creativity on the frontlines. So how did he manage to keep so many leaders moving forward together?

One brief but compelling set of rules embedded in the minutes of the Methodist conference opens the window into Wesley's strategy for aligning leadership. These guidelines or principles, called "The Rules of a Helper," are Wesley's response to the challenge of providing leadership for this growing movement. These rules were formative as Wesley mobilized the first few volunteers who joined him in leading this rapidly expanding enterprise, and these rules were invaluable as he deployed thousands of lay leaders first in the British Isles, then globally, to advance this great cause.

It is telling that few of the early Methodists were managers or leaders in business or community organizations. Leadership was not a topic of study in any academic setting. No leadership seminars or best-selling books covered the topic. Most of these "helpers" had never served in any leadership capacity outside of their own homes. Wesley's critics were not always impressed with his choice of co-laborers. Augustus Toplady, best known for his hymn "Rock of Ages," was one of Wesley's fiercest opponents. He accused Wesley's team of "prostituting the ministerial function to the lowest and most illiterate mechanics, persons of almost any class, but especially common soldiers. . . . Let his cobblers keep to their stalls. Let his tinkers mend their brazen vessels. Let his barbers confine themselves to their blocks and basons [sic]. Let his bakers stand to their kneading-troughs. Let his blacksmiths blow more suitable coals than those of controversy."[6] Yet today, Toplady is remembered for one hymn while Wesley is remembered as the leader of the vast Methodist movement. Wesley grasped something about leadership in God's kingdom that eluded Toplady. He knew that God does not always call the equipped, but God will not fail to equip the called.

Jesus, too, called everyday people like fishermen and tax agents to join his leadership team. There was no shortage of priests in Jerusalem, whom Jesus might have recruited. Instead, he selected his team from among people working hard to make a living in the marketplace. Wesley did the same. He recruited soldiers and bakers who had experienced a changed life through God's grace. He gave women a meaningful place of leadership in the Methodist societies and enterprises long before they were given the right to vote.

However, Wesley did not simply give people a title and send them on their way. Early on he recognized the need to provide direction and boundaries to his team members for the work they would undertake on his behalf. Clear expectations were essential then and today.

"Rules of a Helper" was first recorded in the minutes of the 1744 conference. This list of rules, in various editions and forms, has endured as a rich source of guidance to leaders for almost three hundred years. But there seems to be only limited awareness of these rules in contemporary Methodist circles. To my knowledge, *Lead Like Wesley* is the first published effort to drill down for the underlying leadership principles that are embedded in these rules.

Wesley was no leadership guru, but I suspect that he would have written more extensively on leadership if he was alive today. He was a prolific writer on a wide range of topics. There is no reason to doubt that he would have added his voice to the many who write on leadership in our generation.

WESLEY CREATED A LEADERSHIP PIPELINE

To be clear, Wesley was not focused on creating a leadership development organization. He was laser-focused on accomplishing the mission of "spreading scriptural holiness over the land."[7] Leadership development was a means, not the end. These rules of Wesley's are not exhaustive. He could have given his leaders much more direction. But what he did provide as counsel in his day endures in our own. It merits our careful consideration.

Wesley modeled leadership. He did not offer theories from an ivory tower. He was engaged in the front lines of the Methodist movement. Wesley understood that while you can impress people from a platform, you impact them only by stepping into their world and modeling the behavior you expect from them.

Leadership theorists refer to this concept as "transformational leadership." Wesley certainly qualifies as a transformational leader.

Against incredible odds, he challenged the status quo and empowered others to join him in a movement that deeply influenced the spiritual climate and culture of a nation. Wesley was not interested in passing along tips, tricks, or five easy lessons to become a better leader today. His purpose in writing about leadership was to assist his helpers toward becoming leaders worth following. He had little patience with those who used titles of positional authority to exert their will over others. Wesley had his fill of people holding ecclesiastical titles but lacking the spiritual and moral authority that inspired others to follow.

Wesley made high demands on his leaders. Those who led one or more class meetings each week were also to meet every Tuesday night with their direct supervisor for accountability and training. Those appointed as circuit riders were expected to travel tirelessly for weeks at a time, leaving behind the comforts of home and family. Any compensation for their labor would generously be described as a living wage. To those who accused him of being authoritarian, Wesley replied,

> It is nonsense, then, to call my using this power, "shackling free-born Englishmen." None needs to submit to it unless he will; so that there is no shackling in the case. Every preacher and every member may leave me when he pleases. But while he chooses to stay, it is on the same terms that he joined me at first. . . . All I affirm is, the preachers who choose to labour with me, choose to serve me as sons in the gospel. And the people who choose to be under my care, choose to be so on the terms they were at first.[8]

No leadership challenge is more daunting than that of leading a volunteer organization. Business leaders can offer financial inducements for cooperation. Military leaders can ensure compliance with the threat of court martial. Leaders in volunteer organizations have few carrots and fewer sticks. The individuals they serve can be motivated only by the organization's mission, a sense of personal fulfillment from making a contribution, and the value of relationships within the organization.

Wesley's method of developing leaders was to entrust them with responsibility. A prospective leader would be put in charge of one group. If that went well, the leader might be entrusted with another group. Those who served well became assistants, supervising the work of class leaders in a particular community. Those who had exceptional speaking gifts were enlisted as preachers and dispatched to the far corners of the movement. Eventually, Wesley deployed Francis Asbury and Thomas Coke to America, entrusting them with oversight of the Methodist movement flourishing in the New World.

Wesley found leaders more open to learning after they had encountered the fires of adversity. He regularly called for conferences in which he and a team of leaders would discuss their experiences and what they had learned in the various fields to which they had been appointed.

Wesley was a voracious reader. He modeled the principle that leaders are readers. His approach to leadership was deeply impacted by what he read of Thomas à Kempis, William Law, Richard Baxter, and others. Likewise, Wesley expected his team to make continuing education a high priority. When asked, "Why is it that the people under our care are no better?" Wesley replied, "Other reasons may concur; but the chief is, because we are not more knowing and more holy." The follow-up question was, "But why are we not more knowing?" Wesley responded,

Because we are idle. We forget our very first rule, "Be diligent. Never be underemployed a moment. Never be triflingly employed. Never while away time; neither spend any more time at any place than is strictly necessary."

I fear there is altogether a fault in this matter, and that few of us are clear. Which of you spends as many hours a day in God's work as you did formerly in man's work? We talk—or read history, or what comes next to hand. We must, absolutely must, cure this evil, or betray the cause of God.

But how? . . . Read the most useful books, and that regularly and constantly. Steadily spend all the morning in this employ, or, at least, five hours in four-and-twenty.[9]

A few of Wesley's team members must have been reluctant to follow his instructions on reading. To those who protested, "But I have no taste for reading," Wesley bluntly replied, "Contract a taste for it by use, or return to your trade."[10]

WESLEY HAD HIGH EXPECTATIONS

For Wesley, other than the direct providence of God, the rise and fall of the Methodist movement depended chiefly on the strength of its leadership corps. If the people in the movement were to keep growing, the leaders must keep growing.

He insisted that the leaders of the movement keep growing in grace. Wesley was adamant that they give high priority to spiritual growth and development. Nurturing their own spiritual vitality was a responsibility that could not be delegated to others. Wesley spoke frequently on the need to work out our salvation, to persist in the pursuit of a holy heart. This was not to earn salvation but to give full expression to the salvation so freely received by the grace of God.

The apostle Peter put it this way:

His divine power has given us everything we need for a godly life through our knowledge of him who called us by his own glory and goodness. Through these he has given us his very great and precious promises, so that through them you may participate in the divine nature, having escaped the corruption in the world caused by evil desires. For this very reason, make every effort to add to your faith goodness; and to goodness, knowledge; and to knowledge, self-control; and to self-control, perseverance; and to perseverance, godliness; and to godliness, mutual affection; and to mutual affection, love. For if you possess these qualities in increasing measure, they will keep you from being ineffective and unproductive in your knowledge of our Lord Jesus Christ. But whoever does not have them is nearsighted and blind, forgetting that they have been cleansed from their past sins. Therefore, my brothers and sisters, make every effort to confirm your calling and election. For if you do these things, you will never stumble, and you will receive a rich welcome into the eternal kingdom of our Lord and Savior Jesus Christ. (2 Pet. 1:3–11)

The apostle Peter said it twice for emphasis: "Make every effort." This especially applies to leaders who accept responsibility to ensure the well-being of the people serving with them.

People sometimes ask, "Are leaders born or are they made?" An exhausting amount of research has been done in search of an answer. The majority of research concludes that innate factors (such as temperament or talents) may orient people toward leadership, but leaders are shaped the most by their life experiences (for example, family dynamics and early opportunities to lead) and what they learn from those experiences. Whatever your starting point, you can improve as a leader. You can cultivate skills and practice behaviors that make you more effective in your role. You can invite feedback and welcome coaching to deal with blind spots that hinder your progress.

John Wesley fervently believed that God's people should keep growing in grace. However, he did not believe in improvement by osmosis. Growth in grace would require effort. "No idleness can consist with growth in grace. Nay, without exactness in redeeming the time, you cannot retain the grace you received in justification. . . . Let him [who] is zealous for God and the souls of men begin now."[11]

The fact that you are reading this book is a positive demonstration of your desire to become a better leader. Whether you are doing this on your own or with a group of leaders, read slowly and reflect on these "Rules of a Helper." My hope is that you will learn along with me from the leadership principles John Wesley offered to his generation. There is little debate that Wesley was a purposeful, if imperfect, leader. What else explains the fact that this Methodist movement endures centuries after his death?

Walter Lippman (1889–1974), an American journalist and political commentator, said, "The final test of a leader is that he leaves behind him in other men the conviction and the will to carry on."[12] That is the true test of a leader. Will the people we lead carry on the mission after we leave the stage? Will we leave a legacy? Wesley passed that test with flying colors. You can too. Thank you for joining me in this discovery of the timeless leadership lessons in John Wesley's "Rules of a Helper." Let's learn to lead like Wesley.

BACKGROUND

Wesley's original version of "Rules of a Helper" may be found in *The Works of John Wesley*, volume 8, available online and from a number of publishers. The rules are included in their entirety in appendix A of this book. Several versions of the list have been revised and updated by various branches of the Methodist family.

Some of the more recent versions of these rules either edit or leave out Wesley's counsel to only "converse sparingly and cautiously with women; particularly, with young women."[13] While leaders are still wise to establish appropriate boundaries with members of the opposite sex, Wesley's language reflects a vantage point that was more relevant to his original readers.

Wesley's fourth rule, "Take no step toward marriage, without first consulting with your brethren,"[14] wisely values the counsel of our fellow leaders, but matters of the heart were not Wesley's strongest point. Given the changing perspectives from eighteenth-century England to today, this rule is omitted from some recent versions. For example, the Methodist Discipline of South Africa updated the original rule 3 to read: "Be guarded in your conversation and friendships lest you be led into temptation" and revised rule 4 to read: "Take no step towards marriage without solemn prayer to God, and consulting your colleagues."[15]

The Wesleyan Church of North America revised the list by excluding the third and fourth rules. Their revised and renumbered list forms the framework for this book.[16] You will notice that each chapter is introduced by a phrase that, for me, best captures the principle behind the rule. I used those key words to help me reflect on and begin to apply these rules to life. As you read and consider Wesley's rules, you may find another key word to be more applicable. You may be the one closer to being right, and I would welcome your feedback. My hope is that you will benefit from the substance of Wesley's practical guidance without being distracted by the frame in which I placed it.

One other consideration in writing this book may be helpful to state here. Wesley used some words differently than we do today. A simple example is the word *wanting*. We usually define *wanting* to mean "longing for" or "desiring." Wesley used the word *wanting* to mean "that which we lack." I trust that you, my intrepid reader, will become familiar with Wesley's antiquated language. My attempts at updating or paraphrasing his vocabulary seemed to be more confusing than clarifying, so I chose to let Wesley speak in his own words. If a particular phrase in Wesley's quotes seems especially confusing, you may find it helpful to consider it in its full context. Searchable editions of Wesley's works are available online for free.

A basic understanding of the structure of the Methodist movement is helpful to better understand the genius of Wesley's leadership methods. Early Methodism was similar to what we would now call a parachurch organization, existing alongside but not officially a part of the formal church. There are whole volumes written on this topic, but here is a simple explanation of the organization's structure. From the converts and spiritual seekers awakened under the preaching of the itinerant evangelists, Methodists gathered in groups of fifty or more called *societies*, which were open to both men and women and met weekly, usually on Sunday evenings, for practical preaching and teaching. Members of each society were required to participate in a *class*, a group of ten to twelve men and women who met weekly for fellowship and encouragement. Classes functioned similar to today's small groups. *Bands* were even smaller groups that were something like accountability groups. Bands were segregated by gender, age, and marital status and met weekly for "close conversation." The Methodist system included other groups as well, including *penitent bands*, which were much like today's recovery groups, and *select societies*, which were very small groups of Methodists, hand-picked for leadership training. By the time of Wesley's death, there were as many as 135,000 members in Methodist societies and more than 500 itinerant preachers.

Wesley's task in formulating these rules was to develop leaders who could help create and sustain a movement of spiritual transformation. These enduring rules have helped shaped the Methodist movement for more than 250 years. Join me as we learn more about what it means to lead like Wesley.

1

LEAD
DILIGENTLY

Make every moment count.

"Be diligent. Never be unemployed a moment.
Never be triflingly employed. Never while away time;
neither spend any more time at any place than is strictly necessary."

John Wesley's "Collection of Prayers," first printed in 1733 and revised through the years, included this reflection question to be considered every Monday morning: "Am I resolved to do all the good I can this day, and to be diligent in the business of my calling?"[1]

Diligence. This is the same word that the apostle Paul used in writing to Roman believers, encouraging them to invest themselves fully in serving with the gifts God had given them: "If it is to encourage, then give encouragement; if it is giving, then give generously; if it is to lead, do it diligently; if it is to show mercy, do it cheerfully" (Rom. 12:8).

According to Albert Barne's commentary, the word *diligence* "properly means *haste* (Mark 6:25; Luke 1:39), but it also denotes *industry, attention,* [and] *care* (2 Cor. 7:11). 'What carefulness it wrought in you' (2 Cor. 7:12); 'That our care for you in the sight of

God' (Rom. 8:7–8). . . . It means here that they should be attentive to the duties of their vocation [and] engage with ardour in what was committed to them to do."[2]

Wesley wanted to make every day count in serving Christ. He avoided long conversations, even with friends, believing that these lengthened talks gravitated toward unprofitable topics or even to gossip. Wesley's most distinguished dinner hosts were surprised to find that he usually excused himself after an hour. Wesley pointedly asked his leaders about their use of time: "Do not you converse too long at a time? Is not an hour commonly enough? Would it not be well always to have a determinate end in view; and to pray before and after it?"[3]

REDEEM THE TIME

John Wesley considered time management a serious responsibility and part of Christian stewardship. He believed this so deeply that he wrote an entire sermon on the subject entitled "On Redeeming the Time." In it, Wesley went into great detail about the amount of sleep a Christian should need. He concluded, from his observation and personal experiments, that men need at least six hours of rest and women needed closer to seven hours.[4]

His own consistent practice was to be in bed by ten in the evening and to arise promptly at four in the morning. To sleep more than necessary was, in his view, to deprive the Lord of the hours needed for worship and productive labor. Wesley went so far as to say that sleeping beyond what is needed for sound health is a sin against God.

Whether you agree with Wesley on this specific point or not, you must concede to his larger argument: Every minute is precious. The twenty-four-hour treasure called today is equally distributed to rich and poor, to diligent and slothful. Wesley wanted every minute to count.

For the past few years, I have kept an index card on my desk that asks this question: What is the next step I can take to move closer to my goal? Another way to frame that question is this: What is the most important thing I can do right now to help fulfill my life calling?

One of the best things about leadership is that there is always something more you can do to better serve your organization. One of the worst things about leadership is that there is always one more thing you can do, so the temptation to hurry is omnipresent. It is always possible for leaders to stay busy, but always being busy can result from failing to focus.

Time is a treasure leaders must steward wisely. Few positions in any organization allow more discretionary time than that of leader. A diligent leader has no trouble finding something to do. The bigger question is whether that leader is doing the most important work that only he or she can do. Effective leaders are not slackers. They tend to arrive earlier and stay later than the rest of the team. They also have tremendous flexibility in the use of the time entrusted to them. They can choose to be incredibly effective with that time. But, if not careful, they can also find themselves wasting time on low-priority projects as easily as a lower-level employee wastes time on social media.

CHOOSE HIGH-IMPACT ACTIONS

Peter Drucker, the father of modern management theory, emphasized the need for diligence in his best-selling book *The Effective Executive*.[5] He made the case that improving time management is essential to a leader's effectiveness. Here are the key points I gleaned from his book:

- Know where your time goes. Without awareness of your current practice, you will not be able to make the needed adjustments for greater effectiveness.
- Eliminate unproductive activities.
- Delegate productive activities to people who can do them as well or better.
- Free up and focus your best time for activities with the highest value to the organization.

Drucker's counsel proved useful in helping me to prioritize my time in my three major leadership roles:

- Lead pastor at New Hope Church in Williston, North Dakota (1992–1998),
- District Superintendent for Wisconsin (1998–2000) and West Michigan (2000–2010), and
- President of Kingswood University (2010–2015).

In each of these roles, I learned that my most significant contributions were: (1) clarifying, modeling, and casting the vision for the organization; (2) recruiting, developing, and encouraging the leaders; and (3) cultivating and aligning the resources with the mission.

Funding the mission is always a priority for a leader, especially in churches and other nonprofit organizations. What differed in each of my three roles was the range of activities required to achieve our funding goals. For example, at New Hope we raised the largest portion of our funding through the congregation's weekly donations. That was adequate until we faced a relocation project. Weekly donations would not close the gap between our regular giving and the added cost of purchasing property and constructing a new worship center. We needed significant pledges from some and additional generosity from all to make this possible. We launched a capital campaign that nearly doubled our annual income over the next three years and enabled us to relocate far sooner than we'd thought possible.

When I moved to a new assignment, leading a statewide association of churches, I was not responsible for personally increasing weekly donations in each congregation. My role was to ensure that we had maximum cooperation from the leadership teams in those churches. They wrote the monthly checks to the district and made it possible for us to reach the annual budget that their delegates had approved.

Leading a network of geographically dispersed churches meant my opportunity to influence any one congregation was limited. I no longer had the privilege of teaching and working with the same group of people every week. The key was to unite the congregational leaders around a vision and key priorities. Both in Wisconsin and West Michigan, we concluded that developing next-generation leaders and planting new congregations were essential priorities for which the district team would be primarily responsible. My principal contribution was to communicate a clear vision and to align our existing resources with that vision. By doing so, we were able to triple our results in church planting.

Later, I led a small Christian university during a highly challenging era for post-secondary education. Clarity of vision is essential in any organization, but for this specific school, managing our way out of a fiscal crisis was the top priority. Lowering costs and raising the level of financial support became my primary focus. Unlike the local congregation, where weekly donations are the bread and butter, colleges depend on annual fund campaigns and capital project donations from alumni and friends. Preaching an annual sermon series on tithing to the college students would not produce the funding we needed to reduce our indebtedness or balance our budget. We had to make sure our graduates succeeded in their new responsibilities and became goodwill ambassadors for the university. Improving our connections with alumni and friends was critical.

Fund-raising events and direct mail initiatives played a large role in raising our support level. Direct donor solicitation was also critical to our organization's fiscal health.

The leadership principles were similar in each role, but my activities varied in each context. The first challenge in being diligent as a leader is to be clear about which activities will add the most value. The second challenge is to allocate premium time to those activities.

CHOOSE WHAT NOT TO DO

Take a few minutes to identify the three activities you're responsible for that contribute the most value to the organization you currently serve. What percentage of your time do you spend on these high-priority activities? If you looked at your schedule like it was an investment portfolio, which tasks would be yielding the highest return on investment?

Vilfredo Pareto (1848–1923), an Italian economist, is best known for observing a phenomena that is now commonly termed the "Pareto principle." This principle is rooted in his observation that 80 percent of the effects in any endeavor can be attributed to 20 percent of the causes. This is commonly known as the 80:20 rule. For the purpose of our conversation, the Pareto principle would indicate that 80 percent of your results come from 20 percent of your activities. To apply this principle, you first have to be clear about the results you want to achieve. You must be equally clear about the activities that most closely correlate with those results. Once you've established the most effective 20 percent of activities, the challenge is to give the greatest percentage of your time to them.

In order to focus on your highest priority, highest impact tasks, you will have to say no to many other good, desirable, even important opportunities and tasks. Dick Wynn, former president of Youth for

Christ USA, was a good friend and mentor to me. He often shared the story of a learning encounter he had with Peter Drucker, the management theorist and educator mentioned earlier. At the close of the seminar, Drucker asked Wynn and the other executives present to consider what they had learned during their time together, and to list the new activities they would implement upon returning to their organizations. Wynn said his own list was long, and most of the other leaders easily filled two or three pages with action steps.

Then Drucker gave the class a more difficult assignment. He directed them to make another list, this one identifying the activities and tasks they would stop doing so they would have time to do the things they had just identified as higher priorities. Wynn said the room grew quiet and hardly a page was turned. While all the executives acknowledged that they couldn't just keep adding more things to their already full schedules, deciding what to let go of was much harder than deciding what to add.

Lead diligently. Identify what you do that adds the most value to your organization. Eliminate unnecessary and low-priority activities. Keep the main thing the main thing. Make every day count.

John Wesley both modeled and taught the importance of leading diligently. Adam Clarke, beloved commentator and protégé of John Wesley, passed along what he had learned from Wesley in this advice to a young friend: "The grand secret is to save time. Spend none needlessly: keep from all unnecessary company; never be without a praying heart, and have as often as possible a book in your hand."[6] Even the songs of early Methodism communicated the need for diligence. Charles Wesley, John's brother and partner in ministry, captured these thoughts in his hymn "Give Me the Faith Which Can Remove":

I would the precious time redeem
And longer live for this alone,

To spend, and to be spent, for them
Who have not yet my Savior known;
Fully on these my mission prove,
And only breathe, to breathe Thy love.

My talents, gifts, and graces, Lord,
Into Thy blessed hands receive;
And let me live to preach Thy Word,
And let me to Thy glory live;
My every sacred moment spend
In publishing the sinner's friend.[7]

Legendary basketball coach John Wooden said, "A leader's most powerful ally is his or her own example."[8] The most compelling reason to lead diligently is that people are following in our footsteps. We will inevitably reap what we model for our team.

One Sunday in May 1760, Wesley attended the morning service at the Church of England in Newry. Following the worship service, he learned that very few people attended the afternoon prayer service held in the church. Wesley's response? "I resolved to set them the example, and the church was full in the forenoon. Of what importance is every step we take, seeing so many are ready to follow us!"[9] Wesley knew the power of example, as did missionary-physician Dr. Albert Schweitzer. He said, "Example is not the main thing in influencing others. It is the only thing."[10]

Diligence matters because the mission matters. The leader's consistency in doing the right thing sets the standard that others on the team will use as the measure of their own diligence. Thomas J. Watson, Sr., former chair of IBM, observed that "nothing so conclusively proves a man's ability to lead others as what he does from day to day to lead himself."[11]

LEAD DILIGENTLY

Dr. Anthony Graham leads New Hope Family Worship Center, an incredible congregation doing effective ministry in the urban core of New York City. When he planted the church with just twelve members, the small congregation could not afford a full-time minister. So Graham taught in the public school system and carried on his pastoral responsibilities during the early morning hours and late into the evening.

The church grew rapidly under Graham's gifted preaching and visionary leadership, and the church board offered him a full-time salary if he would leave his teaching position. Graham prayed about it but clearly felt led to continue teaching while providing leadership to the church. He asked the board to instead employ an assistant who could cover administrative tasks and oversee the church's daily operations. The board agreed, and the church continued to flourish under this arrangement.

In time the church grew to the point where it could afford both the assistant and a full-time salary for Graham. He again declined and redirected the funding into additional staffing. This happened several times, and each time Graham was convinced that God had placed him in the public education system to be a positive influence, and there were others who could be meaningfully deployed in the ministry.

I had the privilege of preaching at New Hope Family Worship Center the weekend Graham celebrated his fiftieth birthday. That Sunday began with a first service at eight in the morning on their main campus in Brooklyn. We then drove to the church's Coney Island site for a second service at ten, then returned to the main campus for the final service of the morning. I was humbled that day when I saw how Graham led this dynamic congregation of more than eight hundred people while continuing to teach full time. This gifted leader also serves on the board of trustees at Houghton College and on the national governing board for his denomination. He accepts invitations to speak internationally and across America and still finds time for his responsibilities as a loving husband and proud father of a growing family. How could he do all of that? Anthony Graham leads diligently. The leaders in his congregation are keenly aware of his willingness to do whatever it takes to accomplish the mission, and his example is both inspiring and contagious. Parishioners rise to the challenge of his example.

Ronald Heifetz, author and Harvard leadership professor, makes a compelling case that "attention is the currency of leadership. Getting people to pay attention to tough issues rather than diversions is at the heart of strategy."[12] Leaders do that best by example. The leader's diligence is one of the best ways to capture the team's attention. How we invest our time and energy is the most easily observed measure of what we believe matters most in our organization. Lead diligently.

REFLECTION

1. Do I view diligence, especially in management of my time, as an act of worship and stewardship before God?

2. In what ways could I improve the way I plan and track my use of time?

3. Which activities or inputs yield the greatest value for my team and for the results we are trying to achieve?

4. What do I need to stop doing so I can do more of what is most important?

2

LEAD
URGENTLY

Take your mission seriously.

"Be serious. Let your motto be, 'Holiness to the Lord.'
Avoid all lightness, jesting, and foolish talking."

This is the second of Wesley's leadership rules that are focused on self-management. His call to lead diligently insisted that his leaders focus on doing the right things. His call to lead urgently asked them to lead seriously, with full intensity and engagement.

It is possible to do the right things without generating momentum in your organization. The people you lead are bombarded with messages that compete for their attention. *The New York Times* reported data from Yankelovich, a market research firm, that people living in cities now receive up to five thousand messages a day, compared with two thousand in the 1970s.[1] How do you capture attention amid this distraction? Leading with a sense of urgency is one way to break through the clutter. If diligence is about focus, urgency is about pace. Lead like what you are doing matters, and it matters now.

Keith Drury, who mentored generations of youth ministry leaders, often said that the three key words for success were these: *Do it now.* Procrastination undermines productivity. If you are serious about what you're doing, get on with it. Work with a sense of urgency. Decide faster. Act faster. Moving faster creates momentum in the leader and the team.

TAKE YOUR WORK SERIOUSLY

Wesley's letter to Mr. James Bogie captures this sense of urgency: "It is an excellent plan: The sooner you put it in execution, the better; only see that you be all punctual to follow one another exactly. Let not a little hindrance or inconvenience put you out of your way—suppose a shower of rain or snow. Press on! Break through! Take up your cross, each of you, and follow your Master: So shall the world and the Devil fall under your feet."[2]

Perhaps you have heard this principle: What is important is seldom urgent, and what is urgent is seldom important. This axiom emphasizes the value of taking time out for planning and other valuable activities that are often crowded out of a leader's daily schedule.

Wesley was not opposed to planning, but he believed that what was most important was also most urgent. He seldom suffered from "paralysis by analysis." Instead, he had what management guru Tom Peters calls "a bias for action."[3] Leading urgently is leading with focused intensity. Wesley was not looking for frenetic energy in his leaders. He was calling for the directed energy that creates and sustains momentum in organizations.

Wesley's critics, and even some friends, cautioned him against being too zealous. In response to one correspondent, Wesley wrote about his sense of urgency:

I detest all zeal which is any other than the flame of love. . . .
I sincerely thank you for endeavouring to assist me herein, to
guard me from running into excess. I am always in danger of
this, and yet I daily experience a far great danger of the other
extreme. To this day, I have abundantly more temptation to
lukewarmness than to impetuosity, to be a saunterer *inter sylvas
Academicas* [Latin for "among the shades of academic groves"],
a philosophical sluggard, than an itinerant preacher. And, in
fact, what I now do is so exceeding little, compared with what
I am convinced I ought to do.[4]

Wesley argued that the greatest temptation for leaders was not in
leading with too much urgency, but in drifting into complacency.
He was more concerned about lukewarmness in his own life, and in
his helpers, than an excess of zeal.

In the early 1760s, Wesley came to be deeply concerned about the
lack of growth in the Methodist societies in Scotland. His correspondence with Christopher Hopper, another Methodist leader, carried this
sense of urgency: "I am much inclined to think you will be more useful this year than ever you have been in your life. From the first hour
abate nothing of our rules, whether of society or bands. Be a Methodist
all over. Be exact in everything. Be zealous; be active. Press on to the
one thing, and carry all before you. How much may be done before
summer is at an end! . . . I hate delay. 'The King's business requires
haste!'"[5] In other words, Wesley said, your mission is serious, and you
should be too. Leaders set the tone for the team with their own sense of
urgency. "But you should keep a clear mind in every situation. Don't be
afraid of suffering for the Lord. Work at telling others the Good News,
and fully carry out the ministry God has given you" (2 Tim. 4:5 NLT).

John Kotter, a Harvard business professor, made a compelling case
from his research that the primary reason organizations don't change
is a lack of urgency. If the leader doesn't demonstrate a sense of

urgency, there is little hope that his or her followers will. Kotter explains that information will not motivate people to change unless it is "sent by someone with confidence, credibility, passion, conviction, or a highly visible sense of urgency."[6]

To create a sense of urgency for individuals and organizations, the leader must model this at every opportunity. Is the stated need for urgency congruent with the actual degree of urgency with which the leader tackles the mission? Does the leader demonstrate urgency in even simple things like starting meetings on time? Does the leader exemplify urgency by eliminating low-priority activities from his or her schedule to make room for higher-value initiatives?

Kotter concludes that "it is often only a steadily growing wave of people behaving with real urgency each and every day that can conquer built-up cynicism and negativity—a real urgency that can start with one person, then two, then ten, and on."[7]

"A steadily growing wave of people behaving with real urgency each and every day" was exactly what Wesley longed to see in the Methodist movement. He understood that the only way to make that a reality was for Methodist leaders to model that urgency every day.

Jim Collins and his team have provided wonderful insights in their books *Built to Last* and *Good to Great*. Collins observes that great companies are "full of people who display extreme diligence and a stunning intensity."[8] Our world would be dramatically different if every Christian leader and every Christian organization were characterized by "extreme diligence and stunning intensity." The early Methodist movement gives us a brief glimpse of what that might look like.

Wesley understood that the level of urgency in the movement would never outpace the level of urgency in its leaders. "Catch on fire with enthusiasm and people will come for miles to watch you burn," is an aphorism often attributed to John Wesley. I was unable to verify that Wesley did in fact write those words, but they accurately reflect his own sense of urgency.

DEVELOP A PASSION FOR SOULS

Wesley knew that the archenemy of urgency is complacency. Writing to one of his leaders, he expressed his disappointment about the apathy he observed in him: "I am concerned for you; I am sorry you should be content with lower degrees of usefulness and holiness than you were called to."[9] Leading urgently maximizes your potential in service to a great cause. There is no greater cause than the mission of God. The Great Commission is of utmost importance and deserves our greatest sense of urgency. Jesus said, "We must quickly carry out the tasks assigned us by the one who sent us. The night is coming, and then no one can work" (John 9:4 NLT).

Jesus spoke of his disciples as workers in the harvest field (see Matt. 9:37–38). At least three things are true about a harvest: (1) It will not gather itself; (2) it has great value; and (3) the time for harvest is limited and therefore requires urgent action. Ripe fruit must be harvested as soon as possible. Left alone, the harvest does not become riper; it spoils. There is no time for delay. Kingdom workers are marked by this sense of urgency.

Some researchers have questioned whether a sense of urgency can be developed in leaders. One wrote, "After over two decades of coaching leaders it is my opinion that many leadership traits can be taught. Some though cannot, and a sense of urgency in my opinion cannot be coached. It is either part of your DNA or not. It is how people are wired."[10] Wesley would disagree. Some experts may have difficulty coaching urgency in executives at chemical companies or financial corporations. Yet Wesley would argue that when the mission is compelling enough, when the stakes are high enough, when the time is short enough, urgency is the only appropriate response.

Wesley wrote to one Methodist society member, "O make the best of every hour!"[11] To another he wrote, "Are you still making the best of life? Employing a few days exactly in such a manner as you judge is most to the glory of God? . . . Happy and wise, the time redeem, and live, my friend, and die to Him."[12] Does your mission matter? Do you take your leadership responsibilities seriously? If you don't, who will?

BE CHEERFULLY SERIOUS

Don't confuse taking your mission seriously with taking yourself too seriously. Even amid the urgency of work that truly matters, it is both possible and helpful to have a positive and cheerful disposition. John Wesley, writing to a new believer in London, instructed her to "let not the liveliness of your spirit lead you into levity: Cheerful seriousness is the point you are to aim at."[13] Cheerful seriousness. That was not an oxymoron for Wesley. Instead, that phrase captures the mind-set Wesley modeled. Christian leaders should not have a gloomy, pessimistic outlook, or be fearful and anxious. The leader in this mission has hope. There is a buoyancy of spirit arising from faith-fueled optimism. Christian leaders have discovered that the fruit of the Spirit includes joy.

Wesley could agree with the apostle Paul, who said, "We are hard pressed on every side, but not crushed; perplexed, but not in despair; persecuted, but not abandoned; struck down, but not destroyed" (2 Cor. 4:8–9). The apostle Paul would later state, "I am greatly encouraged; in all our troubles my joy knows no bounds" (7:4). That is remarkable. Paul experienced hardship as he pressed the battle, but he also experienced joy. Leading urgently should not produce a scowl. Christian leaders can display urgency with a song in their hearts and a smile on their faces.

People appreciate a positive attitude in their leaders. Winston Churchill's indomitable spirit in the face of overwhelming odds inspired confidence in the British people during World War II. A quotation often attributed to him states, "For myself I am an optimist— it does not seem to be much use to be anything else."[14]

Leading with cheerful seriousness does not make you a comedian. Stand-up comics are among the best-known entertainers in our culture, but they are seldom looked to for leadership. People appreciate a leader with a sense of humor. That is especially true when a leader uses humor to acknowledge his or her own foibles. But the leader who takes nothing seriously is not taken seriously.

A friend of mine, whom I'll call Edward, is one of the funniest and most fun-loving guys I know. He lightens up every room he enters. But he realized that people were not taking him seriously as he moved into higher levels of leadership. The same humor that endeared him to so many as a first-level supervisor was not as helpful when he found himself representing the entire organization in high-stakes meetings. So Edward learned to tone it down. While he is still a fun person to spend time with, he has became more selective about using humor.

I served with another leader who used humor to control and sometimes even humiliate people. He was quick-witted and sharp-tongued. People did laugh with him, but others expressed regret at the way that he used humor to dominate others. This leader was one of the most gifted I ever worked with, and he rose to prominence in international circles. But his circle of influence grew smaller as the number of those he belittled grew larger.

Daniel Goleman and his team of researchers provide invaluable insight for leaders in their book *Primal Leadership*. One of their findings is that "the artful use of humor typifies effective leadership." Goleman's team interviewed a sampling of leaders, including a number of top executives in American and international corporations. The leaders who had been previously identified as outstanding were also those who scored significantly higher in the use of humor. The research revealed that the effective leaders "used three times more humorous comments—about one every four minutes—than the average leaders. The most effective leaders, then, use humor more freely, even when things are tense, sending positive messages that shift the underlying emotional tone of the interaction."[15]

The key is to find balance. None of these executives were auditioning for the comedy club circuit. They took their businesses seriously, and their people took them seriously. They simply understood and leveraged the value of humor in leadership settings.

Wesley's sense of humor comes through in his journals, though in the dry, British style. He observed an Irish wake at which professional wailers were present: "I was exceedingly shocked at (what I had only heard of before) the Irish howl which followed. It was not a song, as I supposed, but a dismal, inarticulate yell, set up at the grave by the four shrill-voiced women, who (we understood) were hired for that purpose. But I saw not one [who] shed a tear; for that, it seems, was not in their bargain."[16] It is interesting both that Wesley made the humorous observation that tears weren't in the mourners' contract and that he retained that note when the journals were published. It is not altogether surprising that contemporary research validates the wisdom of Wesley's cheerful seriousness. Culture has changed, but human nature remains intact.

Wesley urged leaders in the Methodist movement to take themselves and their mission seriously. He welcomed cheerful seriousness but urged his team members to avoid frivolity or levity. They should not aspire to become entertainers or comics. Their mission was too important to risk being marginalized or trivialized by indiscriminate joking or playing the clown.

BE DRIVEN BY MISSION

Ultimately, Wesley called leaders to focus with intensity on the mission. His teaching on this topic is often summarized in a famous quote for which he is credited, though there is no evidence that he ever said it: "Do all the good you can, by all the means you can, in all the ways you can, in all the places you can, at all the times you can, to all the people you can, as long as ever you can." Though there is no record that Wesley made that statement, he did model it. That statement communicates the urgency that marks the man or woman who leads like Wesley. There is much good work to be done for God and for others, and there is no time to waste.

In the winter of 1747, Wesley was trying to make his way from Stilton to keep an appointment in Grantham when the innkeeper's servant warned him against setting out that morning: "Our servant came up and said, 'Sir, there is no traveling today. Such a quantity of snow has fallen in the night, that the roads are quite filled up.' I told him, 'At least we can walk twenty miles a day, with our horses [being led] in our hands.' So in the name of God we set out."[17]

When Wesley had completed the twenty-mile journey, he discovered that the foul weather had kept others from venturing out to hear him. Not one to waste an opportunity, Wesley rested for an hour and then set out for Epworth, traveling another twenty-four miles in the storm before reaching Newark and taking lodging for the evening.

Wesley made the most of every opportunity. But even he admitted that he did not do all he could. Writing to one of his critics, Wesley confessed that he was ashamed before God for his inactivity: "I do not spend all my time so profitably as I might, nor all my strength; at least, not all I might have, if it were not for my own lukewarmness and remissness; if I wrestled with God in constant and fervent prayer."[18]

J. Oswald Sanders, in his classic book *Spiritual Leadership*, quotes J. H. Jowett, an outstanding church leader of a previous generation:

> I think one of the cant phrases of our day is the familiar one by which we express our permanent want of time. We repeat it so often that by the very repetition we have deceived ourselves into believing it. It is never the supremely busy men who have no time. So compact and systematic is the regulation of their day that whenever you make a demand on them, they seem to find additional corners to offer for unselfish service. I confess as a minister, that the men to whom I most hopefully look for additional service are the busiest men.[19]

I found this to be true during my tenure as president of Kingswood University. Most often, it was our best students, as measured by their academic performance, who also invested themselves in leading the college's spiritual and community life. It was a rare occasion when a top student complained of being too busy doing homework to join in serving others. Unfortunately, students who most often complained about not having enough time to serve found plenty of time to play video games or hang out in the student lounge. They missed the sense of urgency captured by the quotation attributed to Richard Baxter, the beloved Puritan pastor, who explained, "I preach'd, as never sure to preach again, and as a dying man to dying men!"[20]

Wesley's journal records his visit in May 1774 to the languishing Methodist work in Glasgow, Scotland. The entry emphasizes the necessity of urgency in the leader: "How is it that there is no increase in this society? It is exceeding easy to answer. One preacher stays here two or three months at a time, preaching on Sunday mornings, and three or four evenings in a week. Can a Methodist preacher preserve either bodily health, or spiritual life, with this exercise? And if he is but half alive, what will the people be?"[21]

Wesley strongly believed that early morning preaching profited both the preacher and the people. There was nothing better to start the day than to gather out of doors to hear a challenging message before heading off to a day of living for Christ in the marketplace.

Wesley's own sense of urgency was consistent, even to the point of interrupting dinners where he was the invited guest. One such evening was in the home of Dr. Leigh, in Halifax, England. A messenger arrived from a nearby village, where the vicar wanted Wesley to come preach to their Sunday evening service. Wesley borrowed his host's horse and a servant to accompany him. He set out immediately, and "riding fast, came into the church while the vicar was reading the Psalms. It was well the people had no notice of my preaching till I came into town: They quickly filled the church. I did not spare them, but fully delivered my own soul."[22] Urgency matters, whether you are a Christian excelling in the marketplace, a leader of a volunteer committee, a founder of a humanitarian relief agency, or a pastor of a church that needs revitalization.

Dr. Nina Gunter, retired general superintendent for the Church of the Nazarene, received the following affirmation of faith from Louise Robison Chapman, who served as a missionary to Africa from 1920 until 1940. Chapman described this as the written testimony of a young pastor in Zimbabwe who was later martyred for his faith. John Wesley would certainly resonate with the urgency of its message:

I'm a part of the fellowship of the unashamed. The die has been cast. I have stepped over the line. The decision has been made. I'm a disciple of His and I won't look back, let up, slow down, back away, or be still. My past is redeemed. My present makes sense. My future is secure. I'm done and finished with low living, sight walking, small planning, smooth knees, colorless dreams, tamed visions, mundane talking, cheap living, and dwarfed goals. I no longer need preeminence, prosperity, position, promotions, plaudits, or popularity. I don't have to be right, or first, or tops, or recognized, or praised, or rewarded. I live by faith, lean on His presence, walk by patience, lift by prayer, and labor by Holy Spirit power. My face is set. My gait is fast. My goal is heaven. My road may be narrow, my way rough, my companions few, but my guide is reliable and my mission is clear. I will not be bought, compromised, detoured, lured away, turned back, deluded or delayed. I will not flinch in the face of sacrifice or hesitate in the presence of the adversary. I will not negotiate at the table of the enemy, ponder at the pool of popularity, or meander in the maze of mediocrity. I won't give up, shut up, or let up until I have stayed up, stored up, prayed up, paid up, and preached up for the cause of Christ. I am a disciple of Jesus. I must give until I drop, preach until all know, and work until He comes. And when He does come for His own, He'll have no problems recognizing me. My colors will be clear![23]

In his letter to Miss Bolton dated August 8, 1773, Wesley encouraged her to press on with urgency: "Life is short! We have need to improve every moment!"[24] Make the most of every moment; that is the essence of this urgency.

John Valton was one of Wesley's workers who had leadership gifts and a growing sense of God's calling. In 1769 Wesley wrote to Valton as he was seeking God's direction for service. Although Wesley did not believe the time had come for Valton to leave his current station, he gave him this encouragement: "And stay where you are as long as you can; but do not resist, when he thrusts you out into his harvest. . . . At present you are to do all you can where you are, and to be always hearkening to his voice, and waiting till he makes plain the way before your face."[25]

Even when we are not yet where we think we are ultimately going to be in our leadership journey, leading with urgency demands that we make the very best of every opportunity presented to us. The advice to "do all you can where you are" remains just as relevant today as it was in 1769. The leader who demonstrates intensity and passion in his or her current assignment is more likely to be considered for larger responsibilities. Jesus taught that the one who is faithful in minor responsibilities will eventually be entrusted with more (see Matt. 25:23).

LEAD URGENTLY

Leadership expert Stephen Covey proposed a matrix to help leaders discern where they currently invest their time and energy. He suggested that every task falls into one of four quadrants:

1. Not urgent, and not important.
2. Urgent, but not important.
3. Important, but not urgent.
4. Urgent and important.[26]

The window on the back door has smudges from the children's last game of tag. It will go on the to-do list, but if the Final Four basketball tournament is on, cleaning that window will probably not qualify as either important or urgent (quadrant 1). The trash is piled high and should be taken out. Given the unpleasant odor, the task may be urgent. But in the grand scheme of things it is not that important (quadrant 2). It is time to check the battery on the smoke detector. You can't remember the last time you replaced it. No one notices. No one is complaining. But if the battery is too low, a fire could spread quickly through the house undetected. Checking the battery and replacing it if necessary may not be urgent, but it is important (quadrant 3). If there actually was a fire in the house, getting the children out would be both urgent and important (quadrant 4). At such moments, we don't worry much about smudges on the window or overflowing garbage cans. Rescuing the lives of family members is vital, and everyone understands and acts on that priority. What about the smoke detector battery? It's easy to forget but vitally important.

Smudged windows and other minor nuisances in an organization can distract leaders. Those matters need to be addressed, but they are never the highest priority for the leader's time. The leader's job is to identify the tasks in quadrant 4 that are most important and the tasks in quadrant 3 that are most urgent. Leaders can, by their example of focused urgency, clarify for the entire team which issues deserve highest priority in time and energy.

In his book *Spiritual Leadership*, J. Oswald Sanders shares this poem on urgency:

> No trifling in this life of mine;
> Not this path the blessed Master trod;
> But every hour and power employed
> Always and all for God.[27]

Richard Baxter (1615–1691), a Puritan pastor, advised, "Spend your time in nothing which you know must be repented of. Spend it in nothing on which you might not pray for the blessing of God. Spend it in nothing which you could not review with a quiet conscience on your dying bed. Spend it in nothing which you might not safely and properly be found doing if death should surprise you in the act."[28]

One of Wesley's best-known quotes is this one from a December 10, 1777, letter to a member of the Methodist society: "Though I am always in haste, I am never in a hurry." Wesley went on to explain,

"I never undertake any more work that I can go through with perfect calmness of spirit. . . . When I was at Oxford, and lived almost like a hermit, I saw not how any busy man could be saved. I scarce thought it possible for a man to retain the Christian spirit amidst the noise and bustle of the world. God taught me better by my own experience."[29]

You are called to serve in the greatest cause of all. What you do for Christ and for others will last into eternity. Give your best to the Master. Lead with cheerful seriousness. Lead urgently!

REFLECTION

1. Would those I serve say that I lead with cheerful seriousness?

2. In what ways do I demonstrate a sense of urgency?

3. What is the overall level of urgency for our team?

4. What changes can I make in how I lead that will clearly communicate to my team our need for greater urgency?

3

LEAD
POSITIVELY

Look for the best in everyone.

"Believe evil of no one; unless you see it done, take heed
how you credit it. Put the best construction on everything. You
know the Judge is always supposed to be on the prisoner's side."

Wesley's first two leadership principles focused on self-leadership. Leading diligently and leading urgently are within our control. In this third rule, Wesley turned the spotlight on how a leader deals with people on the team. Wesley understood that self-management is a foundational skill for all leaders, but not everyone is self-motivated. If they were, our job as leaders would be a lot easier.

How then do you lead those around you? Wesley instructed his helpers to begin by believing the best about their team members. He encouraged leaders to give their people the benefit of the doubt. That was even more important when someone was being criticized or attacked. Wesley stressed that the leader must consider the accused innocent until proven guilty. For me, the real gem in this rule is found in this statement: "Put the best construction on everything."[1]

John Wesley would not succeed on today's motivational speaker circuit. He wrote no best sellers on the power of positive thinking. He was not an extroverted, sanguine personality who whistled his way through life, blissfully unaware of its heartaches and trials. Wesley was a steely eyed realist who knew the stakes and counted the cost in the face of fierce, sometimes violent, opposition. He and other leaders in the Methodist movement were attacked, stoned, and beaten. They were constantly subjected to mockery and frequently cursed at as they carried out their mission.

In spite of all of this, Wesley could say with the apostle Paul, "Therefore we do not lose heart. Though outwardly we are wasting away, yet inwardly we are being renewed day by day. For our light and momentary troubles are achieving for us an eternal glory that far outweighs them all. So we fix our eyes not on what is seen, but on what is unseen, since what is seen is temporary, but what is unseen is eternal" (2 Cor. 4:16–18).

BE HOPEFUL IN ALL CIRCUMSTANCES

This third principle applies primarily to a leader's responses to other people, but leading positively is not confined to interpersonal relationships. It would be unusual to find a leader who is negative and pessimistic about everything else in life but upbeat and optimistic when dealing with people. We would be just as surprised to find a leader who was gracious in dealing with all other challenges in life but unkind and unforgiving with colleagues.

Wesley certainly proves that case. His general outlook on life was positive, whether dealing with people or the everyday hardships of constant travel. He chose to be content in all circumstances (see Phil. 4:11–13). He would agree with Dr. Charles Swindoll's conclusion: "The single most significant decision I can make on a day-to-day basis in my choice of attitude. It is more important than my past, my education, my bankroll, my circumstances, or my position. . . . The longer I live the more convinced I become that life is 10 percent what happens to you and 90 percent how we respond to it."[2]

Wesley chose to react to life's challenges with a firm conviction that God was at work in all things. Wesley had plenty of reasons to give up, but he pressed on with faith even when the circumstances did not support his optimism. Like many speakers and preachers, Wesley preferred a responsive audience, which he described as warm. But whether his audience was warm or cold, Wesley believed God was at work so he pressed on: "I preached at noon to a warm congregation at Loddon, and in the evening to a cold one at Yarmouth. I know there is nothing too hard for God; else I should go thither no more."[3]

One of Wesley's most trusted colleagues was Mr. Ebenezer Blackwell. Blackwell was the principal partner in a London bank and maintained a country residence a few miles outside the city. Blackwell's estate in Lewisham was a place where Wesley could relax and write during gaps in his rigorous schedule of itinerant preaching. Blackwell was entrusted with much of the banking for the charitable work of Wesley's United Societies. Many of Wesley's letters to Blackwell concerned the administration and distribution of these funds. But the letters almost always included notes of encouragement as well.

Wesley wrote Blackwell from Bristol in February 1747 with banking instructions and a report of the growth of the United Societies across Ireland and England. As one example, Wesley noted that the society in Leeds had grown from one hundred eighty to more than five hundred members. Then Wesley concluded with this thought: "And shall you have no part in the general blessing? I believe better things. You will fight and conquer; take up the cross till you receive the crown. You have both been enabled to set your faces heavenward; and you shall never look back."[4]

Wesley was not naïve about the cost of following Jesus, especially in the marketplace. But he always viewed these difficulties through the prism of God's grace and framed the difficulties in the light of eternity. This perspective shines through Wesley's brief note to Mr. Blackwell in 1755: "What a blessing to have these little crosses, that we may try what spirit we are of! We could not live in continual sunshine. It would dry up all the grace of God that is in us. . . . Let us fight the good fight of faith together, and more resolutely lay hold on eternal life!"[5]

Wesley's journal records many circumstances of difficult weather and unpleasant accommodations during his travels. Here is one example from his ministry visit to Ireland in 1775: "In the night the rain came plentifully through the thatch, into my lodging-room. But I found no present inconvenience, and was not careful for the morrow."[6] He refused to let a leaky roof ruin a good night's sleep or his plans for the next day. Consistently choosing a positive attitude is the expression of a grateful heart.

In a longer letter later that same summer, Wesley explained how he practiced this positive, optimistic approach, which he called "good humor," in a variety of circumstances:

I am content with whatever entertainment [lodging and hospitality] I meet with, and my companions are always in good humour, "because they are with me." This must be the spirit of all who take journeys with me. If a dinner ill dressed, a hard bed, a poor room, a shower of rain, or a dirty road, will put them out of humour, it lays a burden upon me, greater than all the rest put together. By the grace of God, I never fret. I repine at nothing: I am discontented with nothing. And to have persons at my ear, fretting and murmuring at everything, is like tearing the flesh off my bones. I see God sitting upon his throne and ruling all things well. . . . This I want, to see God acting in everything, and disposing all, for his own

glory, and his creature's good. I hope it is your continual prayer, that you may see him, and love him, and glorify him with all you are and all you have![7]

One lesson from this letter is that if you purpose to stay positive and optimistic, you must surround yourself with people who share that same spirit. Negativity is contagious. Wesley was clear: "Good humor . . . must be the spirit of all who take journeys with me." That is good advice for leaders. Be wise in selecting the people you spend your time with. Ride with people who share your positive spirit.

Wesley's commitment to see the best in every situation rose from his belief that God is at work in even the small details of life, something he called "particular providence." Wesley wasn't an optimist simply because he had a good temperament. His perspective on life, with its ups and downs, was formed by his belief in a gracious God. His peace in the middle of storms, his joy in the face of opposition was the overflow of the work of grace God was doing in his life.

Returning to Tullamore, Wesley experienced a more positive response to his ministry than he'd had in a previous visit. Commenting on that change, he wrote, "Why should we ever be discouraged by the want of present success? Who knows what a day may bring forth?"[8] Wesley lived positively and led positively.

BELIEVE THE BEST OF OTHERS

Leadership is ultimately about the heart. Leadership is about finding and developing the best in others. To do that, we have to understand that people's hearts are hardwired to respond to hope.

Dan Reiland, executive pastor at 12Stone Church, said it this way: "Being a positive person is essential to effective and sustained leadership. . . . Our primary disposition among the people we lead cannot be negative. We must live in a way that causes people to be drawn toward us and lifted up. . . . Good leaders are not afraid to confront important issues. But the reception to those difficult talks is usually more positive when the leader is known to be an encouraging, positive, and uplifting person."[9]

Pessimists make exceptional painters and poets. They do not make good leaders. The leader deals in large-scale hope for the future of the organization. That is what we commonly call vision. But the leader also deals in hope for the individual. This belief that each individual can contribute to the greater good is essential. People need to know that their leader believes in them.

John Maxwell, a Wesleyan minister and best-selling author on the subject of leadership, put it this way: "It is wonderful when the people believe in the leader. It is more wonderful when the leader believes in the people."[10] Wesley's passionate preaching and relentless pursuit of the mission attracted a growing number of followers. But it was his belief in people that enabled Wesley to mobilize the leaders needed to sustain a movement that continues to this day. That belief was key to developing leaders from coal miners and carpenters to bankers and housewives. Wesley really believed ordinary people, with God's grace and good leadership, could make a difference. People believed in Wesley. Their belief in him produced crowds. Wesley believed in people. His belief in them produced a movement.

Wesley agreed with the apostle Paul's assertion that love always looks for the best in people: "If you love someone, you will be loyal to him no matter what the cost. You will always believe in him, always expect the best of him, and always stand your ground in defending him" (1 Cor. 13:7 TLB).

DEFAULT TO TRUST

One way to lead positively is by entrusting the people you lead with responsibility and empowering them with authority. Wesley had high expectations and clear guidelines for his team members, yet he allowed for significant latitude in the execution of plans. Wesley sent directions to a Mr. Hopper to resolve a conflict at the Methodist orphanage and promised to fully support Hopper's decisions: "Act just the thing that is right, whoever is pleased or displeased. I hereby give it under my hand, I will stand by you with all my might."[11]

Hopper received a letter from Wesley the following year with this encouraging message: "I am much inclined to think you will be more useful this year than ever you have been in your life."[12] Wesley was not naïve about the human condition. He knew that his leaders failed sometimes. When that happened, he was more than willing to confront them, a practice outlined later in these rules for leaders.

One such setback had occurred in the life of a colleague identified only as T. R. In a letter to Thomas Rankin, Wesley noted, "I am sorry for poor T. R. It is certain God did lift up his head; and I had hoped that his besetting sin would no more have dominion over him. However, you must in nowise give him up. And he has much more need of comfort than of reproof. His great danger is despair."[13] Even though T. R. had failed, Wesley was not ready to give up on him. Instead, Wesley encouraged Rankin to comfort T. R. and seek his restoration.

Wesley looked for the best in others and was unwilling to believe otherwise unless proven before his own eyes. One gentleman, with whom Wesley spoke in the summer of 1757, had inconsistently answered his call to leadership. The man had first taken up with the Moravians but later fallen out with them. Then he became a deacon with them again. Finally, citing points of conscience, he withdrew from their fellowship once more. Finally the man brought his case to Wesley. Rather than simply believe the criticisms given by others, Wesley agreed to hear him out. "I had much conversation with Mr. ——; whom, against a thousand appearances, I will believe to be an honest, though irresolute man."[14] The very next day, Wesley invited him to be present for the annual conference of the United Societies. Wesley did not allow the negative opinion others might have of an individual to determine how he would deal with that person.

Mark Miller worked in leadership development in the corporate sector for many years. His experience confirms this principle: "When you expect the best from people, you will often see more in them than they see in themselves."[15]

REFUSE TO MALIGN CRITICS

It is one thing to be positive when people are applauding and quickly following your lead. It is more difficult to believe the best about people when they fail to follow through on their commitments. Believing the best about those who oppose and criticize you may be the ultimate test of your attitude.

One of Wesley's longest correspondences was with an anonymous critic who wrote by the not-so-imaginative pen name of Mr. John Smith. Wesley's careful responses to Mr. Smith's charges and accusations comprise almost fifty pages of his published works. Notice the gracious, optimistic tone of Wesley's responses:

1. I was determined, from the time I received yours, to answer it as soon as I should have opportunity. But it was the longer delayed, because I could not persuade myself to write at all, till I have leisure to write fully. And this I hope to do now, though I know you not, no, not as much as your name. But I

take for granted that you are a person that fears God, and [who] speaks the real sentiments of his heart. And on this supposition I shall speak, without any suspicion or reserve.

2. I am exceedingly obliged by the pains you have taken to point out to me what you think to be mistakes. It is a truly Christian attempt, an act of brotherly love, which I pray God to repay sevenfold into your bosom. Methinks I can scarce look upon such a person, on who is "a contender for truth and not for victory," whatever opinion he may entertain of me, as an adversary at all. For what is friendship, if I am to account him my enemy who endeavours to open my eyes, or to amend my heart?[16]

The footnotes to this letter, in the 1872 edition of Wesley's *Works*, conclude that the anonymous Mr. Smith was none other than Dr. Thomas Secker, then bishop of Oxford, who later became the archbishop of Canterbury. Wesley never revealed whether he eventually discovered his opponent's identity, but this positive response to criticism raises the bar for anyone who aspires to lead like Wesley.

Laurel Buckingham, my mentor and friend, leads positively. He looks for the best in people. Nothing captures his perspective on people better than this favorite statement: "I suffer from inverse paranoia. I believe everyone is out to do me good."

Wesley was determined to lead positively whether responding to critics or bearing up under the disappointment of unreliable colleagues. John Hutchinson, one of the Methodists, had, by his own confession, been in a long revolt from God. Here again, Wesley never gave up hope of Hutchinson's recovery to full relationship with God: "It is much easier for me to hope than to despair of any person or thing. I never did despair of John Hutchinson. For with God no work is impossible."[17]

Another coworker, Thomas Maxfield, caused Wesley some distress over doctrinal issues. Wesley, while fully aware of the likely end of the matter, continued to look for the best possible outcome: "If Thomas Maxfield continues as he is, it is impossible he should long continue with us. But I live in hope of better things."[18] Notice Wesley's heart in that last phrase. He was not naïve about the trajectory of Maxfield's course, but Wesley continued to hope for the best.

Even Wesley's opponents noted his positive approach. This stood out to others, especially when he would refuse to speak unkindly of those who set themselves up as his rivals: "Mr. Wesley is always speaking well of these gentlemen, and they can never speak well of him."[19]

Stephen Covey underscores the value of believing the best about people in his best-selling book *Principle-Centered Leadership*: "Assume the best of others. Assuming good faith produces good fruit. By acting on the assumption others want and mean to do their best, as they see it, you can exert a powerful influence and bring out the best in them. . . . Some may let us down or take advantage of our trust, considering us naïve or gullible. But most will come through, simply because we believe in them. Don't bottleneck the many for fear of a few!"[20] That strikes at the core of leading positively. When you are leading positively, you see the potential in others, usually more than they see in themselves, give them the time and direction they need to develop, and resist the temptation to give up on people too quickly. Covey also quotes Johann Wolfgang von Goethe: "Treat a man as he is and he will remain as he is; treat a man as he can and should be, and he will become as he can and should be."[21]

LOOK FOR POSITIVE OUTCOMES

Early in my ministry, I experienced a significant setback. I was terminated because of an immature and unwise comment that I made in the presence of another staff member. Looking back, I admit that I was an idealistic young adult who specialized in pointing out flaws rather than seeking out solutions. In my youthful idealism, I was unrealistic in my expectations of organizations and the people who led them. Unfortunately, the organization I was serving did not live up to those expectations. When I verbalized my frustration, a coworker interpreted it as disloyalty and reported it to our boss, who formed the same opinion. A few hours later I was called to the boss's office, reprimanded, and fired with two weeks' notice. I was crushed. My confidence was shaken. Several years later I could still recall those feelings of rejection and self-doubt.

The most unfortunate consequence of that experience was how it shaped my outlook on others. I became distrustful. That played out in a variety of ways, most regrettably through a tendency to keep people on a very short leash of trust.

Fast forward to 1992, when I was privileged to lead an exciting congregation in North Dakota. As the church grew, we hired two employees to lead teams of volunteers. I found myself in an awkward relationship with these new staff members. Although I had recruited and hired them, I did not believe in them as fully as they deserved. On two occasions, I responded quickly to negative situations involving these staff members. In both cases, I failed to invest the time needed to rehabilitate or restore. Reflecting on my own termination experience, I decided the wise leader was better off to change the roster than to wait for the players to change.

Firing someone on short notice might play well on reality TV, but it does not make for a healthy organization. My decisions may have been expedient, but I did not serve those individuals well. The church continued to grow despite the jarring transitions. But I could have avoided unnecessary pain for the team members if I had been wise enough to lead like Wesley.

Honestly, after the second firing, I never wanted to hire another staff person again. I knew that wasn't realistic, of course. If our organization was to accomplish our mission, we'd need more team members. But that shows how deeply I was affected first by my own firing, then by the difficult challenge of leading others. I realized that changing players was not always the best solution. I needed to look in the mirror and change the heart of the leader. I continue to work on becoming more trusting, empowering, and encouraging. I want the people who work with me to see a difference between the leader I used to be and the leader I am today.

Believing the best about people is essential to maximizing their potential. Maximizing the potential of team members is the surest way to improve the organization and achieve the best possible results.

James Kouzes and Barry Posner's helpful book *The Leadership Challenge* was required reading in the graduate course I taught at Kingswood University. Their research confirms the value of leading positively:

Believing in others is an extraordinarily powerful force in propelling performance. If you want your constituents to have a winning attitude, you have to do two things. First, you have to believe that your constituents are already winners. It's not that they will be winners someday; they are winners right now! If you believe that people are winners, you will treat them that way. Second, if you want people to be winners, you have to behave in ways that communicate to them that they are winners. . . .

It's a virtuous circle: you believe in your constituents' abilities; your favorable expectations cause you to be more positive in your actions; and those encouraging behaviors produce better results, reinforcing your belief that people can do it. And what's really powerful about this virtuous circle is that as people see that they are capable of extraordinary performance, they develop that expectation of themselves.[22]

My friend Ward Koeser is one of those positive leaders. We served together for six years at New Hope Church in Williston, North Dakota. Ward was the lay leader of the congregation and took me, as a young pastor, under his wing. We met at least once each week during those years and built an enduring friendship. In all the years I have known him, I have yet to hear Ward say a negative thing about another person. He always encouraged the people around him to be their best. He didn't complain when things were not going well in his business. He never stopped seeing the potential in the community, even when so many others left for greener pastures. Eventually, Ward was elected mayor and led the city for twenty years.

During Ward's tenure as mayor, Williston experienced an oil boom and became one of the most prosperous communities in America. Ward was invited to brief Congress, to be interviewed for national television programs, and to host billionaires from around the world. Through the ups as well as the downs, he was the same positive person and found multiple opportunities to share his faith in Christ.

LEAD POSITIVELY

John Wesley believed the best about people and communicated that both by his words and by trusting them with significant responsibilities. One indication of that was his willingness to release all financial management of the movement into the care of stewards. Wesley turned over income from the weekly offerings to these trusted managers, along with all proceeds from his publishing enterprises. Their meticulous accounting records still exist, and they were a strong safeguard against the libelous charges of profiteering sometimes leveled against Wesley.

Wesley's letter to Mrs. Sarah Ryan demonstrates his willingness to believe in people even when others doubted. He delegated full authority over the Methodist household operations in Bristol and the school in Kingswood to Mrs. Ryan in spite of the fact that some of her closest friends did not have that level of confidence in her ability: "Surely God will never suffer me to be ashamed of my confidence in you. I have been censured for it by some of your nearest friends; but I cannot repent of it. Will not you put forth all your strength (which indeed is not yours; it is the Spirit of the Father which now worketh in you) . . . in managing all things pertaining to the house, so as to adorn the gospel of God our Saviour?"[23]

Leading positively begins with believing the best about both people and life in general. This is not naïve optimism but lasting hope grounded in faith. No leaders should be more positive than those who follow Christ. Our optimism is fueled by the firm conviction that "in all things God works for the good of those who love him, who have been called according to his purpose" (Rom. 8:28). Knowing that God is ever at work in us and for us gives us the confidence to lead positively.

REFLECTION

1. How do I demonstrate that I believe in my team members?

2. In what ways have I modeled a positive perspective when faced with opposition or setbacks?

3. Which of my team members most need to be reassured of my confidence in them?

4. Is there someone I have given up on who deserves a second chance?

4

LEAD
CANDIDLY

Treat others with candor and fairness.

"Speak evil of no one; else your word especially would eat as doth
a canker. Keep your thoughts within your own breast,
till you come to the person concerned."

Rules 3, 4, and 5 comprise a triplet of wise counsel for leaders who are responsible for developing the culture of the organization and nurturing the character of team members. Rule 3 encourages a leader to view people in the best possible light, no matter what others may say. Rule 5 directs the leader to intervene when there is a legitimate concern. Rule 4 provides a critical step between the two.

In rule 4, Wesley demands that a leader who has a legitimate concern about someone's behavior never express that concern to others before lovingly and plainly addressing it with the individual. With this rule, Wesley attacks the cancer that has destroyed many organizations. Faultfinding, gossip, slander, or what Wesley called evil-speaking, is not confined to organizations in eighteenth-century England. Businesses, governments, educational institutions, and churches today can still be derailed by an unhealthy organizational culture.

AVOID EVIL-SPEAKING

Churches are especially vulnerable to this breakdown because they place a high value on trust relationships. People come to the church with the expectation that they will find a safe, encouraging community of believers. Unfortunately, those expectations are too often and too easily eroded by gossip or anonymous criticism.

When people are unsure what might be said about them, that lack of confidence will destroy a culture of collaboration. Ultimately, a trust deficit will undermine the mission. Wesley believed that speaking negatively about others had devastating consequences for all concerned. He was convinced that people on the inside of the organization speaking ill of each other could do more damage than any outside critic. He had good reason to feel that way based on his own experience. Wesley was never surprised that irreligious folk, agnostics, or skeptics criticized him. And he fully expected merchants of vice to oppose the transformation that was his aim. Wesley was undeterred by external opposition. What he found unconscionable was internal attacks, the acid of negativity that worked its way through even the ranks of his own organization. Wesley could not abide anonymous attacks and gossip from within the community of faith.

Wesley found this occurring among the Methodists at Kingswood when he arrived there on February 28, 1741. One of the workers he appointed had created serious division by teaching doctrine contrary to Wesley's teaching. The doctrinal deviation by itself was painful enough. Wesley, however, was even more concerned by the gossip and slander that accompanied the controversy. Many of the same people who professed loyalty and approval to Wesley's face mocked and slandered him in his absence.

Wesley met with all the concerned individuals and parties who desired a hearing. He listened closely. Then he acted. Here is what he wrote and then read to them:

By many witnesses it appears that several members of the Band Society in Kingswood have made it their common practice to scoff at the preaching of Mr. John and Charles Wesley: That they have censured and spoken evil of them behind their backs, at the very time they professed love and esteem to their faces: That they have studiously endeavoured to prejudice other members of that society against them; and, in order thereto, have belied and slandered them in diverse instances.

Therefore, not for their opinions, nor for any of them (whether they be right or wrong), but for the causes above-mentioned, viz., for their scoffing at the word and the ministers of God, for their tale-bearing, backbiting, and evil-speaking, for their dissembling, lying, and slandering:

I, John Wesley, by the consent and approbation of the Band Society in Kingswood, do declare the persons above-mentioned to be no longer members thereof. Neither will they be so accounted, until they shall openly confess their fault, and thereby do what in them lies, to remove the scandal they have given.[1]

Notice that those censured were not excluded from the society for their opinions. It was their backbiting and evil-speaking that warranted discipline. Wesley, with typical British understatement, concluded: "At this they seemed a little shocked at first."[2]

The house was already divided. The damage had been done long before Wesley arrived at Kingswood. What remained was to speak the truth plainly and find a way forward. Wesley met again with the society the next Friday evening, March 6, and again on Saturday evening, March 7. He found those opposing him still unwilling to acknowledge the harm they had done or to repent of the part they had played in it. The instigator of the doctrinal division and his followers walked out together that Saturday night.

Wesley gathered the band members together on Sunday night, March 8. He spoke on the Lord's Supper and on the danger of offending with our words. Examining the records that evening, he concluded that the number of those withdrawn was fifty-two persons. The number of those remaining in the now united society was approximately ninety. For those who stayed, Wesley prayed: "O may these, at least, hold 'the unity of the Spirit in the bond of peace!'"[3]

Wesley felt the pain of this division for some time, referring to the memory of it as a "melancholy subject." This would not be the last time that the gossip and slander of friends would wound him. However, it proved a significant learning experience, and he doubled his resolve to warn against the danger of evil-speaking. By 1760 Wesley had written and preached a pointed message on this cancerous behavior. He recommended that all leaders familiarize their people with his sermon entitled "The Cure of Evil-Speaking." In it Wesley went to great lengths to define this relational evil as:

> Neither more nor less than speaking evil of an absent person; relating something evil, which was really done or said by one that is not present when it is related. Suppose, having seen a man drunk, or heard him curse or swear, I tell this when he is absent; it is evil-speaking. . . . Nor is there any material difference between this and what we usually style tale-bearing. If the tale be delivered in a soft and quiet manner (perhaps with expressions of good-will to the person, and of hope that things may not be quite so bad), then we call it whispering. But in whatever manner it be done, the thing is the same — the same in substance, if not in circumstance. Still it is evil-speaking; still this command, "Speak evil of no man," is trampled under foot; if we relate to another the fault of a third person, when he is not present to answer for himself.[4]

COMMUNICATE FAIRLY

Wesley insisted that Methodists not speak ill of or find fault with those who were not present to answer for themselves. He urged the leaders of the bands and societies to use this sermon to tackle this problem of gossip head on: "Read in every society the 'Sermon on Evil-Speaking.' Let the leaders closely examine and exhort every person to put away the accursed thing. Let the preacher warn every society, that none who is guilty herein can remain with us."[5]

Wesley most frequently referenced Titus 3:2—"Slander no one"—in combatting this problem, but there is no shortage of Bible passages that deal with the sin of evil-speaking. While I served as president at Kingswood University, our community fasted at noon on Fridays and gathered for prayer in the chapel. As if to echo Wesley's teaching on this subject, one of the students in our circle read Psalm 15 before we began praying:

> LORD, who may dwell in your sacred tent? Who may live on your holy mountain? The one whose walk is blameless, who does what is righteous, who speaks the truth from their heart; whose tongue utters no slander, who does no wrong to a neighbor, and casts no slur on others; who despises a vile person but honors those who fear the LORD; who keeps an oath even when it hurts, and does not change their mind; who lends money to the poor without interest; who does not accept a bribe against the innocent. Whoever does these things will never be shaken.

David the psalmist was also David the king, a political ruler who had more than his fair share of critics. He had felt the sting of whispered lies. He knew the poisoning effect of slurs and slander. In Psalm 35:15, he wrote, "But when I stumbled, they gathered in glee; assailants gathered against me without my knowledge. They slandered me without ceasing." Again, in Psalm 41, David wrote about his experience with slander saying, "My enemies say of me in malice, 'When will he die and his name perish?' When one of them comes to see me, he speaks falsely, while his heart gathers slander; then he goes out and spreads it around. All my enemies whisper together against me" (vv. 5–7).

Slander was a problem in the New Testament church. The apostle Paul addressed the issue in multiple letters. Notably, Paul included slander in a list of grave moral offenses in his letter to the Corinthian church: "Do you not know that wrongdoers will not inherit the kingdom of God? Do not be deceived: Neither the sexually immoral nor idolaters nor adulterers nor men who have sex with men nor thieves nor the greedy nor drunkards nor slanderers nor swindlers will inherit the kingdom of God" (1 Cor. 6:9–10). Paul placed slanderers squarely in the company of idolaters and thieves. There is no minimizing or trivializing the sinful nature of evil-speaking. The apostle Peter also spoke against this poison that eats away at authentic community in the church: "Therefore, rid yourselves of all malice and all deceit, hypocrisy, envy, and slander of every kind" (1 Pet. 2:1).

The problem of slander was identified in the Old Testament and continued to be addressed by the New Testament church. Wesley was not surprised to find that he had to combat it constantly in the Methodist movement. In his 1772 letter to a young disciple, Wesley made this observation:

Of all gossiping, religious gossiping is the worst: It adds hypocrisy to uncharitableness, and effectually does the work of the Devil in the name of the Lord. The leaders, in every society, may do much towards driving it out from the Methodists. Let them, in the band or class, observe, 1. "Now we are to talk of no absent person, but simply of God and our own souls." 2. "The rule of our conversation here is to be the rule of all our conversation. Let us observe it (unless in some necessarily exempt cases) at all times and in all places." If this be frequently inculcated, it will have an excellent effect.[6]

Wesley encouraged leaders to deal with this sinful behavior head-on, and he provided an example through his own diligent attention to this matter when meeting with each Methodist group. His journal records this the morning after Wesley preached in Reading on Wednesday evening, November 4, 1747: "I began examining the classes, and every person severally, touching that bane of religion, evil-speaking."[7]

Wesley's correspondence to Miss Bishop, more than thirty years later, included a warning about the corrosive danger of evil-speaking. "How does the little society prosper? Are you all united in love? And are you all aware of that bane of love—tale-bearing and evil-speaking?"[8]

Several of John Wesley's sermons touched on this theme, either condemning hurtful conversations or commending more appropriate conversations. For example, his sermon "Repentance of Believers" speaks convincingly against any conversation that does not flow from love:

Indeed it is to be feared, that many of our words are more than mixed with sin; that they are sinful altogether; for such undoubtedly is all uncharitable conversation; all which does not spring from brotherly love; all which does not agree with that golden rule, "What ye would that others should do to you, even so do unto them." Of this kind is all backbiting, all tale-bearing, all whispering, all evil-speaking, that is, repeating the faults of absent persons; for none would have others repeat his faults when he is absent. Now how few are there, even among believers, who are in no degree guilty of this; who steadily observe the good old rule, "Of the dead and the absent—nothing but good!"[9]

BUILD TRUST WITH TRUTH

Trust is created by a combination of factors, but credibility is a foundational element. Can an individual be relied on to do what they say they will do? Credibility is the key to trust, and trust is the currency of leadership.

Speaking negatively about people who are not present sows seeds of mistrust in an organization. When that behavior is tolerated, even the participants are left to wonder what is said about them when they are not present. Even before people find out what was said about them, unspoken cues may signal that interpersonal dynamics on a team have broken down. Simple gestures like rolling the eyes or abruptly halting conversations when another person passes by send the not-so-subtle message that the fabric of trust is unraveling. People inevitably find out what has been spoken about them in their absence. And when they do, what had been a gradual erosion of teamwork quickly becomes a mudslide. The offended person will, understandably, respond somewhere on the flight-or-fight scale. The response can be painful for everyone involved. Adrenaline surges. Tempers flare. One lashes out. Another walks out.

What may be even worse is that in this toxic environment people begin to play it safe. They keep their heads down and their hearts closed. Interpersonal distrust creates an atmosphere of hesitancy, caution, and risk aversion. People suffer—the mission suffers—when gossip and slander are allowed to take root in an organization.

An equally essential but often overlooked ingredient of trust is candor, whether or not the leader and his or her colleagues are completely truthful with one another. Where trust is absent, people are guarded in disclosing information, especially anything that might reflect poorly on them or their work. When trust is lacking, people cooperate to the extent required but are unwilling to extend themselves to help their colleagues. Where trust is missing, people fear rejection by the group and consequences from the leader. Where trust is strong, people communicate freely, collaborate willingly, and risk fearlessly.

Stephen Covey explored the impact of trust on organizations in his book *The Speed of Trust*. He quoted John Whitney, professor at Columbia Business School, saying that "mistrust doubles the cost of doing business," and Jim Burke, former CEO of Johnson & Johnson, saying, "You can't have success without trust. The word *trust* embodies almost everything you can strive for that will help you succeed."[10]

Covey cited a 2002 research study by Watson Wyatt which demonstrated that "total return to shareholders in high-trust organizations is almost three times higher than the return in low-trust organizations." He also pointed to research by Stanford professor Tony Bryk, who found that "schools with high trust had more than a three times higher chance of improving test scores than schools with low trust."[11]

Covey unpacked a total of thirteen behaviors that are vital to building trust in any organization. The first behavior on his list of trust builders is to talk straight. The second most effective behavior is to demonstrate respect. Evil-speaking fails on both counts.

Wesley insisted on straight talk, what he called "plain dealing," and was convinced that confronting people directly, when necessary, was the loving and respectful thing to do. The Bible contains timeless wisdom for leadership and human relationships, none better than that found in Matthew 18. There Jesus outlines the proper way to confront improper behavior. Wesley drew inspiration for his sermon "The Cure of Evil-Speaking" directly from that passage.

SPEAK CANDIDLY

From Scripture, experience, and reason, Wesley was convinced that confronting an individual directly is far more productive than talking to other people about the problem. When appropriate discipline is lovingly applied as prescribed in Matthew 18:15–20, the grace-filled confrontation results both in what is best for the individual and in greater trust within the organization.

Speaking plainly and personally to the person involved in any conflict builds trust. Speaking to others about it is both disrespectful and unloving. Trust is fragile, and gossip is one sure way to destroy it.

Wesley was not one to shy away from saying hard things when necessary. He was never reluctant to hold difficult conversations, but he would not tolerate speaking evil of someone who was not present. When a person is not present to hear the specific grievances against them, he or she is unable to offer a defense, apologize if needed, and amend future behavior. Wesley went so far as to call evil-speaking the "grand hindrance" to brotherly love.

Take Wesley's logic a step further. If the unity of our fellowship is essential for the spread of the gospel, then evil-speaking is the grand hindrance to the growth of the entire Christian movement. This must not be allowed. Wesley was determined that Methodism must be free from gossip in any form: "O that all you who bear the reproach of Christ, who are in derision called Methodists, would set an example to the Christian world, so called, at least in this one instance! Put ye away evil-speaking, tale-bearing, whispering: Let none of them proceed out of your mouth! See that you 'speak evil of no man'; of the absent, nothing but good. If ye must be distinguished, whether ye will or no, let this be the distinguishing mark of a Methodist: 'He censures no man behind his back: By this fruit ye may know him.'"[12] If the Methodists were to be known for anything, Wesley pleaded that it should be their refusal to speak negatively about people behind their backs.

In summarizing his March 1741 intervention at Kingswood, Wesley recorded in his journal, "I told them, open dealing was best; and I would therefore tell them plainly what I thought (setting all opinions aside) had been wrong in many of them."[13]

Wesley's ministry travels in May 1781 brought him to the town of Neath. There he observed the impact of evil-speaking on the Methodist society there: "Some months since, there were abundance of hearers at Neath: But, on a sudden, one lying tongue set the society on fire, till almost half of them scattered away. But as all, offended, or not offended, were at the Town-Hall, I took the opportunity of strongly enforcing the apostle's words, 'Let all bitterness, and wrath, and anger, and clamour, and evil-speaking, be put away from you, with all malice.' I believe God sealed his word on many hearts; and we shall have better days at Neath."[14] One can only imagine the frustration of leaving a thriving society and then returning a few months later to find it divided and dwindling due to gossip.

Wesley opposed evil-speaking in the church, and he argued against it in the political realm as well. After examining Methodist society members on October 3–5, 1774, Wesley instructed them about their voting responsibilities in the upcoming election. His first instruction was to not sell their votes, a frequent practice in that era. His next words may seem surprising to us. Wesley advised the members "to speak no evil of the person they voted against: And . . . to take care [that] their spirits were not sharpened against those [who] voted on the other side."[15]

Such advice was uncommon in Wesley's day and seems more so today. Yet his admonition may be even more critical now, given the twenty-four-hour news cycle and constant bombardment of political opinions through social media. Evil-speaking is a cancer that destroys not only the one spoken about, but also the well-being of the one speaking and of those who consent to listen.

COMMUNICATE OPENLY

The person who speaks slanderously against another must first consider him- or herself to be somehow superior in character to the one he or she accuses. Speaking against someone not present to defend him- or herself is an act of pride, disloyalty, and cowardice. Any issue serious enough to be spoken about with others should be taken directly to the one concerned. If the issue is not serious enough to confront, why spread it to others?

The person who listens to gossip must consider him- or herself above falling into the same pit as the one slandered. Listening to gossip is an act of complicity. Better to bring an immediate halt to the conversation than to tacitly take in the consequential damage to another person's reputation and, ultimately, to the team's united front.

Covey adds this recommendation: "Speak about others as if they were present."[16] Being loyal to those who are absent is one of the surest ways to build trust in the hearts of those who are present.

Why did Wesley make such a point about the power of a few small words? Joel Green in his book *Reading Scripture as Wesleyans* reflects on the special emphasis that Wesley placed on the sin of evil-speaking and makes this observation: "What propelled this text off the pages of the New Testament and into this kind of attention? Undoubtedly, this is due to the premium Wesley placed on genuine Christian fellowship, which included ingredients like truth-telling and accountability."[17]

To be authentically Christian was Wesley's deep longing. From his earliest days in the Holy Club at Oxford, one of his most valued blessings was what he termed "holy conversation." Wesley went so far as to include Christian conference or holy conversations as one of the five "instituted" means of grace through which God works to form his people into Christ's likeness. Wesley listed: (1) prayer,

(2) the Word of God (read, heard, and meditated upon), (3) the Lord's Supper, (4) fasting, and (5) Christian conference. On Christian conference, he wrote, "Are you convinced how important and difficult it is to 'order your conversation right?' Is it 'always in grace? Seasoned with salt? Meet to minister grace to the hearers?' Do not you converse too long at a time? Is not an hour commonly enough? Would it not be well always to have a determinate end in view; and to pray before and after it?"[18]

Wesley was convinced that God-honoring conversations were a powerful means of shaping the character of individuals and of the team. In one correspondence in 1770, he affirmed a man's evident desire to grow spiritually. But in Wesley's view, there was a missing element that would be essential for progress: "Nay, I doubt not but you pant after it now; your soul is athirst to be all devoted to God. But who will press you forward to this? Rather, who will not draw you back? It is in this respect that I think one [who] uses plain dealing is useful for you in the highest degree; so needful, that without this help you will inevitably stop short: I do not mean of heaven; but of that degree of holiness, and, consequently, of happiness both in time and eternity, which is now offered."[19]

Plain dealing is the very antithesis of evil-speaking. Wesley had declared his commitment to speaking plainly even before his Aldersgate experience. In March 1738, John returned to Oxford to be with his brother Charles, who, it was feared, might be dying. During the time that John prayed and waited for Charles to recover, he renewed several resolutions he had written earlier:

To use absolute openness and unreserve, with all I should converse with.

To labour after continual seriousness, not willingly indulging myself in any the least levity of behaviour, or in laughter—no, not for a moment.

> To speak no word which does not tend to the glory of God; in particular, not to talk of worldly things. Others may, nay, must. But what is that to thee? And,
>
> To take no pleasure which does not tend to the glory of God; thanking God every moment for all I do take, and therefore rejecting every sort and degree of it, which I feel I cannot so thank him in and for.[20]

That first resolution, to converse with absolute openness, served Wesley well. For the rest of his life, he was determined to root out evil-speaking wherever he found it in the Methodist movement.

Wesley himself had benefitted from many caring but candid conversations about his own spiritual journey. Plain speaking was a core practice of the band meetings. In fact the fourth rule of the band societies, originally drawn up in December 1738, was "to speak each of us in order, freely and plainly, the true state of our souls, with the faults we have committed in thought, word, or deed, and with the temptations we have felt, since our last meeting."[21] This required a demanding level of authenticity. Such open confession was unlikely to occur in a setting where people could not trust one another. Even one breach of confidence, however small, would undermine the fabric of this confessional community.

In addition to agreeing to speak plainly about their own condition, band members were required to receive feedback about themselves from other members of the group. These were some of the questions that they were to ask each other:

> Do you desire to be told of your faults?
>
> Do you desire to be told all of your faults, and that plain and home?
>
> Do you desire that every one of us should tell you, from time to time, whatsoever is in his heart concerning you?

Consider! Do you desire we should tell you whatsoever we think, whatsoever we fear, whatsoever we hear, concerning you?

Do you desire, that, in doing this, we should come as close as possible, that we should cut to the quick, and search your heart to the bottom?

Is it your desire and design to be on this, and all other occasions, entirely open, so as to speak everything that is in your heart without exception, without disguise, and without reserve?[22]

Wesley and a small group of others had experienced this level of candid and searching conversation under the leadership of Peter Bohler in 1738. The authentic community Wesley enjoyed in that small group significantly shaped his practice in building the small group structure that sustained the Methodist revivals.

Wesley knew that even the words uttered in casual conversations mattered. He counseled believers to follow a "more excellent way" in their dinnertime conversations:

The time of taking our food is usually a time of conversation also; as it is natural to refresh our minds while we refresh our bodies. Let us consider a little, in what manner the generality of Christians usually converse together. What are the ordinary subjects of their conversation? If it is harmless (as one would hope it is), if there be nothing in it profane, nothing immodest, nothing untrue, or unkind; if there be no tale-bearing, backbiting, or evil-speaking, they have reason to praise God for his restraining grace. But there is more than this implied in "ordering our conversation aright." In order to this it is needful. First, that "your communication," that is, discourse or conversation, "be good"; that it be materially good, on good subjects; not fluttering about anything that occurs; for what have you to do with courts and kings? It is not your business to "Fight o'er the wars, reform the state"; unless when some remarkable event calls for the acknowledgment of the justice or mercy of God. You must indeed sometimes talk of worldly things, otherwise we may as well go out of the world. But it should be only so far as is needful: Then we should return to a better subject. Secondly, let your conversation be "to the use of edifying"; calculated to edify either the speaker or the hearers, or both; to build them up, as each has particular need, either in faith, or love, or holiness. Thirdly, see that it not only gives entertainment, but, in one kind or other, "ministers grace to the hearers." Now, is not this "a more excellent way" of conversing?[23]

LEAD CANDIDLY

From the anonymous letters of Wesley's day to bullying on social media in our generation, the destructive power of slander and gossip endures. Christian organizations are not immune from these attacks. While I was serving as president at Kingswood University, our campus was negatively impacted by two or three students who criticized other students and activities at the school in an anonymous online forum. Addressing this nuisance took needless time and energy away from both students and administrators. Ironically, those same students could one day find themselves anonymously criticized while holding a leadership position.

Around the same time we experienced this on our campus, the national news media in Canada reported a rise in cyberbullying through the same online forum that our students had used: "Recently, All Saints Catholic High School in Ottawa sent a note home to parents saying it and other schools 'are experiencing an increased number of issues with respect to negative comments made on social media sites' such as Yik Yak. Nima Naimi, who conducts cyberbullying research at McGill University in Montreal, says the anonymity offered by the app may lead to a lack of empathy and users saying things that they wouldn't normally say in person."[24] Nothing could be less Christian. This behavior is condemned as sinful in both Old and New Testaments. Wesley confronted this devastating conduct in his day. So will we.

While serving as the regional director for a network of churches in Michigan, I saw a pastor and church devastated by a whispering campaign. What might have been expressed early on as legitimate concerns went underground, and eventually those whispers about job performance became attacks on character. Over a period of several months, an atmosphere of mistrust developed as people spoke against the pastor behind his back. Eventually, enough of the talk circulated back to him that he addressed it publicly. The young pastor willingly acknowledged that he made some mistakes. But the damage to his reputation was too great to repair. He resigned. People left the church. Those who remained behind were embittered. The reputation of the church and the cause of Christ took a crippling blow, all because people engaged in evil-speaking.

Anyone who leads people will eventually face the challenge of rooting out gossip, slander, or other forms of evil-speaking. The leader must set the example by refusing to engage in this destructive behavior. The leader must also, as we shall consider in the next chapter, be able to deal firmly and directly with this and other counterproductive behaviors on the team. Few things are more destructive than gossip directed by team members at one another. Failure by a leader to confront evil-speaking in a team is a dereliction of duty. To lead like Wesley, you must create and deepen trust among your team members. Lead candidly.

REFLECTION

1. How would I describe the level of trust and plain speaking in my organization?

2. Am I aware of any evil-speaking in my organization? If so, what can I do to confront it?

3. Have I recently, or ever, participated in gossip or slander? Do I need to repent? Do I need to make amends?

4. What steps can I take to raise the level of trust in my organization?

5

LEAD
RESPONSIBLY

Confront unhealthy behavior lovingly, plainly, and promptly.

"Tell every one what you think wrong in him, and that
plainly, and as soon as may be; else it will fester in your heart.
Make all haste to cast the fire out of your bosom."

Winston Churchill reportedly said, "The price of greatness is
responsibility."[1] Wesley understood that leadership involves taking
responsibility for others. This includes accepting the responsibility
to confront inappropriate behavior in team members or in the team
itself. Good leaders do this lovingly and honestly and quickly. Putting
off the confrontation only makes the situation worse. If improper
behavior is not dealt with promptly, resentment can easily settle into
the leader's heart. Confrontation benefits the leader as much as it
does the team members.

Wesley refused to let unproductive or sinful behavior fester in the
Methodist movement. He was willing to confront it and do so directly.
He knew the stakes were too high. People's lives and eternal destinies
hung in the balance. Wesley expected his leaders to carefully examine
the lives of their class members to ensure that none were turning

away from their commitment to grow in Christlikeness. And he practiced what he preached.

It is essential to capture the three conditions Wesley embedded in this rule:

1. Do this lovingly. Check your heart attitude to make sure your motivation is clear and that you are acting in the other person's best interest and not simply getting something off your own chest.

2. Do this plainly. If you have something hard to say, say it clearly. Don't hint around or make the other person guess what you mean. Don't make assumptions about motives. Stick to the facts.

3. Do it as soon as possible. Don't rush into a crucial conversation in the adrenaline of the moment, but don't delay too long. Sooner is better than later when it comes to confronting and dealing with unproductive behavior.

Wesley's guidance here is priceless. The majority of interpersonal issues that come to a senior leader's desk could be avoided if frontline leaders simply followed this advice.

Most leaders, by personality or temperament, gravitate toward dealing with people either lovingly or plainly. Some of us find it much easier to focus on the relationship when confronting another person. We are better at affirming and encouraging than correcting. Others seem almost to enjoy communicating hard truths but often leave people so discouraged that they give up. Wesley directed leaders to keep the balance between confronting plainly and lovingly. Both are important.

Wesley recorded several occasions when he was personally involved in correcting and seeking to restore a member of the society. One such occasion occurred in Everton on August 1, 1759: "A few of us spoke freely and largely to a brother who had been 'overtaken in a fault,' and endeavoured to 'restore him in the spirit of meekness:' And we were much comforted over him; having great hope that God would restore his usefulness, as well as his strength."[2]

CONFRONT LOVINGLY

John Trembath was an early partner in Methodist ministry, being named as one of Wesley's assistants in 1743. He traveled with Wesley to Ireland in 1747 and was appointed to be the speaker of the day on Tuesday, August 11, for a large congregation gathered at Marlborough Street. Trembath started out well in his leadership journey, but Wesley discovered that a strong start does not guarantee a strong finish. Early success had caused Trembath to become prideful. Wesley learned that Trembath was not living up to the standard expected of a Methodist leader and wrote to him in 1755, appealing to his colleague to remember the days when he was "simple of heart, and willing to spend and be spent for Christ." Wesley feared that much had changed and that Trembath had now "suffered loss by being applauded." Wesley identified two primary concerns: vanity and stubbornness. Wesley called on Trembath to "recover the life of God in [his] own soul and walk as Christ walked." Wesley's rebuke was stern, but he held out hope with this challenge: "You must be much in the way or much out of the way; a good soldier for God, or for the Devil. O choose the better part! Now! Today!"[3]

You might think that would be enough for Trembath to get the message and correct the error of his ways. However, all evidence is to the contrary. Trembath's decline continued to weigh on Wesley. Five years later, Wesley wrote again: "You cannot stand still; you know this is impossible. You must go forward or backward. Either you must recover that power, and be a Christian altogether; or in a while you will have neither power nor form, inside nor outside."[4]

Wesley's letter focused on the heart of the matter: Trembath was content with relying on his elementary lessons and past experiences with God. Wesley understood that team members are unlikely to grow when the leader is not growing. Knowing that learning is essential for a leader's growth, Wesley rightly insisted that his leaders must be readers.

Trembath's lack of prayer, reading, and thoughtful reflection was taking a toll. He was shrinking his own soul and shortchanging the people he was supposed to be leading. Wesley wrote,

> I scarce ever know a preacher read so little. . . . Hence your talent in preaching does not [improve]. . . . You wrong yourself greatly by omitting this. You can never be a deep preacher without it any more than a thorough Christian. . . . Whether you like it or no, read and pray daily. It is for your life; there is no other way; else you will be a trifler all your days, and a pretty superficial preacher. Do justice to your own soul; give it time and means to grow. Do not starve yourself any longer. Take up your cross, and be a Christian altogether. Then will all the children of God rejoice (not grieve) over you.[5]

Wesley's letter demonstrated the spirit of Ephesians 4:15: "Speaking the truth in love, we will grow to become in every respect the mature body of him who is the head, that is, Christ." Wesley wrote to another Methodist leader: "Unless you deal very closely with those committed to your care, you will not give an account of them with joy. Advices and admonitions at a distance will do little harm or good."[6] Wesley confirmed by his own experience the truth taught by King Solomon: "Better is open rebuke than hidden love. Wounds from a friend can be trusted, but an enemy multiplies kisses" (Prov. 27:5–6).

Wesley completed a translation of "Martin Luther's Life," a biography of the Reformer, on July 19, 1749. In reflecting on Luther's life, Wesley wrote these words in his journal: "Doubtless he was a man highly favoured of God, and a blessed instrument in his hand. But O! What a pity that he had no faithful friend! None that would, at all hazards, rebuke him plainly and sharply, for his rough, untractable spirit, and bitter zeal for opinions, so greatly obstructive of the work of God!"[7]

The journal entry underscores the high value that Wesley placed on making yourself accountable to a select group of people who share your spiritual pilgrimage. However, to lead like Wesley does not mean constantly finding fault with others. Continually pointing out the weaknesses or flaws of others is not the way to influence them. In a letter to Reverend Samuel Furley, Wesley shared his own growth in this area: "The longer I live the larger allowances I make for human infirmities. I exact more from myself, and less from others. Go thou and do likewise!"[8]

But Wesley was not reluctant to confront wrong behavior when it was serious enough to negatively impact others. He understood that to be his responsibility as a leader.

CONFRONT PLAINLY

Ken Blanchard and Spenser Johnson wrote a short but helpful book titled *The One Minute Manager*.[9] In it, they described three behaviors essential to creating a productive work environment: one-minute goal setting, one-minute praising, and one-minute reprimands. Of the three, Blanchard and Johnson say the hardest to do well is the one-minute reprimand. Most of us experience enough negativity in life, so we naturally avoid anything that sounds like criticism or looks like confrontation. Conflict avoidance may be a natural tendency, but it is disastrous behavior for leaders and the teams they lead.

Joseph Grenny and his team did extensive research on this topic. Their best-selling book, *Crucial Conversations*, reveals that ineffectiveness in organizations is often the result of leaders failing to confront unproductive behavior: "At the heart of almost all chronic problems in our organizations, our teams, and our relationships lie crucial conversations—ones that we're either not holding or not holding well. Twenty years of research involving more than 100,000 people reveals that the key skill of effective leaders, teammates, parents, and loved ones is the capacity to skillfully address emotionally and politically risky issues. Period."[10]

A leader who allows unproductive behaviors to continue unchecked allows poison to flow through his or her organization's bloodstream. That toxicity may explode without warning, but before it does, it steadily drains the team's energy and effectiveness. Like it or not, the leader has a significant role to play in identifying problems and initiating interventions to address them. That almost always requires "crucial conversations" with key players.

Grenny offers clear directions for making crucial conversations productive. The leader is responsible to ensure that these conversations are conducted in such a way that everyone feels safe and supported. It is not enough to point out the problems. The leader must also point the way forward. Done well, the conversation produces clarity about important issues and may even bring a greater sense of connection between the parties involved.

I have been on both ends of those conversations, and I know it is not easy to initiate a confrontation. The temptation is to avoid it and hope the problem works itself out over time. My experience is that bad situations don't get better over time. They get worse. Someone has to stand up and say something. Ultimately, that is the leader's job.

I have terminated only the two people referenced earlier for cause over the course of my leadership career. In both cases, a series of crucial conversations preceded the decision. As I've said, in hindsight, I might have handled both situations differently. Yet there is no doubt in my mind that something had to be done or our team would have deteriorated. I had to accept ownership for starting those conversations.

I have been fired twice. The leaders who fired me, both of whom I still admire and respect, determined that my performance or attitude did not serve the organization well. They judged that terminating my employment was in the team's best interest. That was their responsibility. They made the best call they knew how to make at the time. I did not enjoy either one of those experiences. However, I learned a lot about myself in the process. I learned even more about what it means to be a leader.

Not every crucial conversation results in someone losing a job. Ideally, crucial conversations take place early enough to lead to a positive outcome. But in every confrontation, the stakes are high.

Dr. H. C. Wilson is a mentor and friend who was one of my early ministry heroes. He planted a church in Halifax, Nova Scotia, that grew to over three hundred people in just a few years. Dr. Wilson went on to serve The Wesleyan Church as a general superintendent, international director of world missions, and district superintendent in both the United States and Canada. I had the privilege of observing his exceptional leadership up close for many years. Dr. Wilson was instrumental in helping me sense and answer a call to vocational ministry. He was my first district superintendent and the general superintendent who officiated my ordination service. Dr. Wilson leads like Wesley. I am grateful for the positive impact of his leadership on my life. One situation will always be especially meaningful to me. It serves as a vivid example of Wesley's fifth rule.

One day Dr. Wilson called to ask if he could stop by my office. I was glad to hear from him and looked forward to seeing him—until I learned the reason for his visit. He came to confront me about my actions, specifically my words, in a recent incident involving another leader with whom we both worked indirectly. He avoided making sweeping generalizations but clearly and directly confronted me about the impact of my words. Though I had spoken with the best of intentions, the impact of my words was negative and Dr. Wilson told me so.

I would love to say that I eagerly welcomed his rebuke, but the truth is that it was quite painful. Not only was it hard to hear this correction from someone I so deeply respect, but I also was not convinced that I had done anything wrong. I am grateful that he persistently and persuasively pointed out where I had been at fault. He was willing to risk our relationship that day not just because he cared about the other leader, but also because he cared about me. He took the responsibility to speak directly to me about my actions, not about me to others. Because he took that initiative, I had the benefit of his objective point of view.

God used that firm but loving rebuke to change my heart and my mind concerning the situation. Dr. Wilson's willingness to have that difficult conversation led me to own my responsibility and take action. As a result, I set up a meeting with our mutual friend. In that meeting, I discovered that my words had indeed hurt this colleague far more deeply than I imagined. I realized that I had failed in my responsibility to create a safe environment where my input might have been better received. I am grateful that Dr. Wilson had the wisdom and leadership to lovingly and plainly confront me.

I attended a seminar with Dr. Laurel Buckingham, my mentor and friend, where he spoke on this topic to a group of pastors in New York. He explained that it was his practice never to respond to a negative incident or a critical letter for at least three days. During those three days, he would pray intently about the situation, seeking God's perspective and checking his heart to make sure that he could respond in love. Then he would take responsibility for finding a solution, no matter who was responsible for the problem in the first place.

Laurel reported that, over the course of more than forty years in pastoral ministry, he could recall only one situation where the other person adamantly refused to be reconciled. In every other case, when he had prayed for at least three days and then responded directly to the person in a loving way, he found that God was able to resolve the problem and, more importantly, restore the relationship.

The underlying principle is that leadership requires accepting responsibility. When a leader assigns blame, that leader abdicates responsibility for finding a solution. When a leader accepts responsibility for the situation, that leader is released from playing the victim and is empowered to move the team toward a solution.

Wesley led by accepting the responsibility to confront. He did so lovingly, clearly, and as soon as possible. Frankly, Wesley sometimes comes across as stern, even severe. That is why I was encouraged to discover a revealing incident in his journal. Wesley recorded his May 1749 interaction with a Methodist society in Ireland that appeared to be struggling spiritually. He wrote, "This day and the next I endeavoured to see all who were weary and faint in their minds. Most of them, I found, had not been used with sufficient tenderness. Who is there that sufficiently weighs the advice of Kempis . . . 'Deal not harshly with one that is tempted.'"[11]

Wesley took the time to ask questions and learn how each person was doing. His diagnosis was that they needed more tenderness. Wesley intuitively knew something that Kouzes and Posner confirmed through their research: "At the heart of leadership is caring. Without caring, leadership has no purpose. And without showing others that you care and what you care about, other people won't care about what you say or what you know."[12]

The familiar maxim expresses it this way: "People don't care how much you know until they know how much you care." It is not enough to have the right answers. You must also have the right spirit. Are you acting in the other person's best interest? Are you sharing with genuine concern from your heart or just getting something off your chest? Writing to Robert Brackenbury, another of his helpers, Wesley reflected, "I have often repented of judging too severely; but very seldom of being too merciful."[13]

Blanchard and Johnson's *The One Minute Manager* explains, "You will be successful with the One Minute Reprimand when you really care about the welfare of the person you are reprimanding."[14] Paul's direction to the believers in Galatia carried that same tone: "Brothers and sisters, if someone is caught in a sin, you who live by the Spirit should restore that person gently" (Gal. 6:1).

CONFRONT PROMPTLY

When Wesley arrived in Nottingham on March 21, 1746, he was discouraged by the lack of vibrancy in the society there. He wrote, "So many of the society were either triflers or disorderly walkers, that the blessing of God could not rest upon them; so I made short work, cutting off all such at a stroke, and leaving only a handful who (as far as could be judged) were really in earnest to save their souls."[15] Wesley took each Methodist's commitment to the society seriously, even if they didn't. He believed it was better to call things the way he saw them than to pretend he didn't see them. He confronted and dismissed those who were not serious about pursuing God's high calling.

Wesley recorded a similar experience with the society in Kemnal, near Norwich, several years later: "I met the society at seven; and told them in plain terms, that they were the most ignorant, self-conceited, self-willed, fickle, intractable, disorderly, disjointed society, that I knew in the three kingdoms. And God applied it to their hearts: So that many were profited; but I do not find, that one was offended."[16]

Wesley insisted on telling people the plain truth. His secret was to do it with so much love that people understood that he wanted what was best for them. God used Wesley's willingness to speak the truth in love at Kemnal, and the day ended on a high note. Wesley was able to conclude that journal entry with these words: "Many stubborn hearts were melted down."[17]

Wesley was convinced not only that a leader must tell the plain truth, but also that it should be done sooner rather than later. That is exactly what Wesley did when calling on a minister in an area where the Methodists had been preaching. "I preached at eight in the place appointed, and thence rode to Dewsbury, where I was to preach at noon. But first I called on the minister, Mr. Robson; and in an acceptable time. Abundance of little offences had arisen, and been carefully magnified by those who sought such occasions. But we both spoke our minds without reserve; and the snare was presently broken."[18]

What a timely meeting that was for Wesley. He had not realized how many little things had been piled up and blown out of proportion. Critics of the Methodists liked nothing better than to build a wall between them and the clergy of the Church of England, and that had doubtless been happening in this case. Wesley and Robson both spoke their minds, holding nothing back, and God worked in that crucial conversation to restore fellowship between two coworkers in the harvest.

Later the same day, after Wesley had preached the noon message in a nearby field, he received a gracious note of invitation from Robson to stop back for another visit. Of that experience, Wesley wrote, "I went and passed such an hour as I have not had since I left London. We did not part without tears. Who knows how great a work God can work in a short time?"[19] Wesley went lovingly, spoke plainly, and did it sooner rather than later. As a result, a strong friendship was rekindled and the work of God was carried on without an unnecessary barrier.

LEAD RESPONSIBLY

Remember John Trembath? Wesley's willingness to confront him eventually paid dividends. Wesley was able to write in 1782, "John Trembath is alive again."[20] Your confrontations may not always lead to a happy ending. However, as a leader, you must accept the responsibility for and learn the skill of confronting unproductive behavior. Years later, John Trembath reflected on his time wandering away from God: "Though God hath forgiven me, yet I cannot forgive myself for the precious time I have wasted, the years I have lost, and the glorious harvest I have neglected."[21] If Wesley had not intervened, it is doubtful that John Trembath would have been restored.

Leadership is responsibility. Leaders take responsibility for themselves, and they accept responsibility for their teams. Leaders embrace the responsibility for accomplishing the mission as their primary objective and the well-being of their team as the primary means.

Dietrich Bonhoeffer wrote, "Action comes, not from thought, but from a readiness for responsibility."[22] Leadership is not a matter of position statements but of accepting responsibility and taking action.

Those of us who are Christ-followers understand the clear connection between our responsibility to God and our responsibility for the others on our team. The writer to the Hebrews pointed out the dual role of leaders in the phrase, "Because [the leaders] keep watch over [the members] as those who must give an account" (Heb. 13:17).

Do not stand back and simply hope that people on your team will work out their own conflicts. Do not expect situations to improve by themselves. Take ownership and take action in the best interests of each member and of the team. Leading like Wesley means leading responsibly.

REFLECTION

1. As the leader, what crucial conversations do I need to have to keep my organization healthy?

2. What was the last situation in which I had to confront a member of the team? Did I confront lovingly? Did I confront plainly?

3. Do I confront as soon as possible? If not, what does that indicate about my tendency toward conflict avoidance or denial? How will I address that?

4. How effectively are others on the team accepting their responsibility to confront lovingly, plainly, and promptly? What can I do to develop this competency in the team?

6

LEAD
HUMBLY

Aim to serve people, not impress them.

Leadership in the church has a different orientation than does leadership in the secular realm. Our example is Christ. Our motivation is gratitude. Our posture is service. "Jesus called them together and said, 'You know that the rulers of the Gentiles lord it over them, and their high officials exercise authority over them. Not so with you. Instead, whoever wants to become great among you must be your servant, and whoever wants to be first must be your slave—just as the Son of Man did not come to be served, but to serve, and to give his life as a ransom for many'" (Matt. 20:25–28).

One of Wesley's significant breakthroughs in organizational management was developing leaders from among everyday people. His primary ministry was among common laborers, and he was not content to stall momentum waiting for ordained clergy to join the cause. He came to appreciate the spiritual gifts and graces that God bestowed on all people regardless of their station in life or academic achievement. Wesley welcomed and valued the contribution of these miners and merchants. Indeed, the Methodist movement would never have achieved its broad impact upon the British Isles without these emerging leaders.

One of the Methodist revival's enduring contributions to British society has been the phenomenon sociological researchers label "redemption and lift." The power of the gospel to truly transform a person, both spiritually and behaviorally, produced a number of positive consequences. People who no longer spent their discretionary time and money drinking and gambling were better able to afford schooling for their children, reading material for themselves, and an overall higher standard of living. People of trustworthy character with settled families and no life-controlling addictions made better employees. Through God's grace and the disciplined lifestyle that characterized the Methodists, they were more likely to be entrusted with responsibilities as shop stewards and in other supervisory positions. The need for qualified people to fill such positions was increasing as the Industrial Revolution created new management structures.

These Methodists were also learning leadership from Wesley. He delegated authority for everything from construction projects and microfinancing enterprises to the spiritual oversight of hundreds of new converts. People flourished in this empowering atmosphere. For many, this was the first time they had been given any leadership opportunity outside of their own household.

The best way to learn leadership is to lead something. Wesley provided a rapidly expanding leadership pipeline through the interlocking network of Methodist societies, classes, and bands. But there was a downside. Wesley entrusted significant responsibility to some individuals who had no previous leadership experience. These new leaders were given a great deal of delegated authority both to speak into the lives of individual members and to direct, in some cases, sizeable Methodist societies in an assigned region. Some emerging leaders handled these responsibilities with grace and humility. Others found it intoxicating and became enamored with their authority to the point of diminishing their influence and dishonoring their office.

A common error in thinking about humility is to confuse it with low self-esteem. C. S. Lewis did not actually write this but he's the most frequently cited source for this balanced perspective: "True humility is not thinking less of yourself; it is thinking of yourself less."[1]

RESIST PRIDE

John Trembath was a talented leader in the early Methodist movement who struggled with humility. I mentioned him in the previous chapter, and his example is useful here as well. Wesley confronted Trembath in a letter, pointing out his lack of humility and its cause: "Not being sufficiently on your guard, you suffered loss from being applauded. This revived and increased your natural vanity."[2] Trembath was one of several early Methodist leaders who fell victim to the temptation the apostle John identified: "They loved human praise more than praise from God" (John 12:43).

Another temptation for leaders, then and now, is to spend time only with people who share the same social circle. Wesley was greatly concerned that upwardly mobile Methodist leaders should not lose touch with the common folk, who needed them the most. Wesley wrote to one young leader:

I want you to converse more, abundantly more, with the poorest of the people, who, if they have not taste, have souls, which you may forward in their way to heaven. And they have (many of them) faith, and the love of God, in a larger measure than any persons I know. Creep in among these, in spite of dirt, and [a] hundred disgusting circumstances; and thus put off the gentlewoman. Do not confine your conversation to genteel and elegant people. I should like this as well as you do: But I cannot discover a precedent for it in the life of our Lord, or any of his apostles. My dear friend, let you and I walk as he walked.[3]

Here was a refined and cultured young woman who was serious about following Jesus. Wesley challenged her personal preference, the natural order of associating only with those of our own social status or above. To walk with Jesus, we must follow where he walked most frequently, with the poor and outcast.

Wesley was conscious of his own vulnerability to pride. Early in life he wrote to a friend about his resolve to go to America in the hope of saving his own soul. He believed that working among the indigenous people would help him escape the many distractions he fought in England. He understood that pride would be the hardest temptation to avoid. He wrote, "If by 'the pride of life' we understand the pomp and show of the world, that has no place in the wilds of America. If it mean pride in general, this, alas! has a place everywhere." Wesley went on in that letter to explain that doing work for which he felt underqualified was a useful step in developing humility. "Nothing so convinces us of our own impotence, as a zealous attempt to convert our neighbor: Nor, indeed, till he does all he can for God, will any man feel that he can do nothing."[4]

For Wesley, humility was seeing oneself correctly, from God's perspective. Few of Wesley's leaders exemplified this trait better than John Fletcher. Wesley admired Fletcher greatly and went so far as to name him as his potential successor in leading the Methodist movement. When Fletcher predeceased him, Wesley deeply mourned Fletcher's death, feeling this as a loss both for the movement and for him personally. Wesley later wrote Fletcher's biography. Among the many noteworthy commendations Wesley gave, none is more convicting than this excerpt, included in Wesley's journal, of Mary Fletcher's description of her husband:

> Not less eminent than his faith was his humility. Amidst all his laying himself out for God, and for the good of souls, he ever preserved that special grace, the making of no account of his own labours. He held himself and his own abilities in very low esteem; and seemed to have that word continually before his eyes, "I am an unprofitable servant." And this humility was so rooted in him, as to be moved by no affront. I have seen many, even of the most provoking kind, offered [to] him; but he received them as his proper portion; being so far from desiring the honour which cometh of men, that he took pleasure in being little and unknown.[5]

These words would be high praise for any person. To receive such a commendation from a friend would be outstanding; it is all the more remarkable coming from Fletcher's spouse. Mary Fletcher wisely observed that patience is the fruit of humility, and that is what she saw consistently in her husband: "From this root of humility sprung up such a patience as I wish I could either describe or imitate. It produced in him a most ready mind, which embraced every cross with alacrity and pleasure. For the good of his neighbour, nothing seemed hard, nothing wearisome."[6]

Mrs. Fletcher was concerned that her interruptions of her husband's writing and study, as often as two or three times in the same hour, would frustrate him. But here again, Fletcher's humility was evident: "He would answer, with his usual sweetness, 'O, my dear, never think of that. It matters not, if we are but always ready to meet the will of God. It is conformity to the will of God that alone makes an employment excellent.'"[7] Fletcher's secret was to see such interruptions as divine appointments. And he was ever conscious that humbly serving God by serving others was the main thing.

Before he died, Fletcher requested that his wife not attend his burial. He understood her need to grieve but did not want others to be kept from hearing the gospel proclaimed because they were distracted by their sympathy for her. She complied with that wish, and she sent written word to the gathered congregation with this testimony to his humility: "He was blessed with so great a degree of humility, as is scarce to be found. I am witness how often he has rejoiced in being treated with contempt. Indeed it seemed the very food of his soul, to be little and unknown."[8]

What a remarkable contrast between Fletcher and John Trembath. Trembath also had great talent and leadership ability, but he loved the crowd's applause so much that he nearly shipwrecked his spiritual life and ministry.

Abraham Lincoln reportedly said, "Nearly all men can stand adversity, but if you want to test a man's character, give him power."[9] The apostle Paul understood that dangerous dynamic and wrote this instruction on selecting leaders to his protégé, Timothy: "He must not be a recent convert, or he may become conceited and fall under the same judgment as the devil. . . . Do not be hasty in the laying on of hands" (1 Tim. 3:6; 5:22). Humility is essential for Christian leadership. Humility is also essential for bringing out the best in others.

FOCUS ON OTHERS

Jeanine Prime and Elizabeth Salib published findings from their international research that identified humility as one of the top four characteristics shared by the best leaders. They quoted Lazlo Bock, senior vice president of people operations at Google, who reported that humility is one of the key attributes he looks for in all new hires. Why is humility so important? Bock explains, "Without humility, you are unable to learn."[10]

Pride hijacks the leader's awareness of the need to seek input from others. Pride also undermines team member's willingness to share what may be crucial information with the leader. If the leader does not invite the contributions of others, no one will give them.

While conducting the research for the book *Good to Great*, Jim Collins and his team tried to minimize the leader's impact on an organization. Despite their best efforts, they could come to no other conclusion: Leadership makes a big difference in every organization.

What Collins's team found enlightening was the *kind* of leadership that contributes to the sustained greatness of an organization. The charismatic, headline-grabbing, self-promoting CEO does not correlate with a company of enduring excellence. Rather, it is the self-effacing but quietly determined leader who develops sustained high performance in a team. About those leaders, whom Collins identified as level 5 leaders, he concluded, "Level 5 leaders embody a paradoxical mix of personal humility and professional will. They are ambitious, to be sure, but ambitious first and foremost for the company, not themselves. . . . Level 5 leaders display a compelling modesty, are self-effacing and understated."[11]

Steve Gutzler, leadership coach and author, reflected on this question, "Why is humility so important for a leader?" Here are his conclusions:

1. It keeps you grounded and focused on serving others.

2. It reminds you that you are but one person, and everyone is important.

3. It allows you to gain and keep the respect of those you are charged to lead.

4. It's the foundation by which all other leadership qualities can thrive.

5. It cuts down pride and keeps you approachable.

6. It's always better to humble yourself than to be humbled.

7. It tells others that you too are a man or woman on a journey, you have not arrived.[12]

One of the most humble leaders I have had the privilege of working with is Dr. Wayne Schmidt. Wayne graduated from Indiana Wesleyan University in 1979 and immediately joined Dr. Dick Wynn in planting a new congregation, Kentwood Community Church, just outside Grand Rapids, Michigan. The church grew rapidly under Wayne's leadership, becoming one of the largest congregations in Michigan. One of the most obvious markers of Wayne's humility as a leader is his passion to keep learning. Even while pastoring a megachurch, he continued his formal education, first at Calvin Theological Seminary and later at Trinity Evangelical Divinity School, where he completed a doctor of ministry degree.

Wayne's humility is publicly modeled but shines in his private life. One example is seen in his commitment to a one-on-one accountability relationship that lasted more than thirty years. Wayne told of bringing his daily diary to put on the table with Paul, his accountability partner. Everything was fair game for Paul's questions, including Wayne's faithfulness in his regimen of proper diet and exercise.

The most striking example, to me, of Wayne's humility occurred in 2009 when he sensed God prompting him to resign as lead pastor of the church he had helped found. Remarkably, he obeyed that leading without having a clear direction as to his next assignment. Very few leaders who are so overwhelmingly loved and respected by their organizations would freely walk away from their position, especially with no next step in sight. Another significant part of that story is how God used Wayne to mentor a younger pastor named Kyle Ray, who became his successor at Kentwood.

I have had the opportunity to observe Wayne closely in multiple settings. He was pastor to my family for several years when I was a member of Kentwood Community Church. He accepted my invitation to join me in the leadership of our regional association of congregations as assistant district superintendent, and we served together for seven years. I had the privilege of being present, along with others, while Wayne processed his decision to entrust the future of the church he had served for over twenty-five years to an inexperienced but God-anointed successor. In each of these settings, I have witnessed his humility as a leader, evidenced by his desire to serve others rather than himself.

It would be inaccurate to leave the impression that Wayne never struggled with pride. Seemingly every leader does. However, I have never worked so closely with a high-capacity leader who so consistently made decisions based on what was best for the mission rather than for him personally. Thomas à Kempis wrote, "The more humble and obedient to God a man is, the more wise and at peace he will be in all that he does."[13] I found that to be true in Wayne's life. People easily notice his wisdom and his contagious sense of peace, and the root of those strengths is humility.

EXAMINE YOUR HEART

John Wesley considered humility so essential that he made it the focus of one full day in his book of prayer. Tuesday was designated as the day for prayers of humility, including these petitions:

Let me learn of thee to be meek and lowly. Pour into me the whole spirit of humility; fill, I beseech thee, every part of my soul with it, and make it the constant, ruling habit of my mind, that all my other tempers may arise from it; that I may have no thoughts, no desires, no designs, but such as are the true fruit of a lowly spirit. Grant that I may think of myself as I ought to think, that I may "know myself, even as I am known." . . . Give me a lively sense that I am nothing, that I have nothing, and that I can do nothing. . . . O save me from either desiring or seeking the honour that cometh from men.

O Lamb of God, who, both by thy example and precept, didst instruct us to be meek and humble, give me grace throughout my whole life, in every thought, and word, and work, to imitate thy meekness and humility. O mortify in me the whole body of pride; grant me to feel that I am nothing and have nothing, and that I deserve nothing but shame and contempt, but misery and punishment. Grant, O Lord, that I may look for nothing, claim nothing; and that I may go through all the scenes of life, not seeking my own glory but looking wholly unto thee, and acting wholly for thee. . . . Give me a dread of applause, in whatsoever form, and from whatsoever tongue, it cometh. . . .

O thou who wert despised and rejected of men, when I am slighted by my friends, disdained by my superiors, overborne or ridiculed by my equals, or contemptuously treated by my inferiors, let me cry out with thy holy martyr [Ignatius], "It is now that I begin to be a disciple of Christ."[14]

Wesley's cultivation of humility went beyond praying about it. His prayer book included an inventory to help Methodists solemnly reflect on their heart's condition and repent of any trace of pride they found:

1. Have I laboured to conform all my thoughts, words, and actions to these fundamental maxims: "I am nothing, I have nothing, I can do nothing"?

2. Have I set apart some time this day to think upon my infirmities, follies, and sins?

3. Have I ascribed to myself any part of any good which God did by my hand?

4. Have I said or done anything with a view to the praise of men?

5. Have I desired the praise of men?

6. Have I taken pleasure in it?

7. Have I commended myself, or others, to their faces, unless for God's sake, and then with fear and trembling?

8. Have I despised any one's advice?

9. Have I, when I thought so, said, "I am in the wrong"?

10. Have I received contempt for things indifferent, with meekness? For doing my duty, with joy?

11. Have I omitted justifying myself where the glory of God was not concerned? Have I submitted to be thought in the wrong?

12. Have I, when contemned, First, prayed God it might not discourage or puff me up; Secondly, that it might not be imputed to the contemnor; Thirdly, that it might heal my pride?

13. Have I, without some particular good in view, mentioned the contempt I had met with?[15]

These questions are challenging but insightful for anyone who aspires to lead like Wesley. A few moments of reflection on questions like these will shine a bright light on any temptation toward pride and other subtle points of disobedience. Prayerfully considering a list similar to this helps me see my heart as God does.

Richard Green's biography of Wesley captures a sense of his humility:

Never was a leader in a great enterprise freer from jealousy of any honour which his coworkers gained. Whitefield, with his spiritualized dramatic power, his self-consuming labour, and his brilliant success; Charles Wesley, not only the chosen hymnist for them all, but a far mightier preacher than he is generally supposed to have been—perhaps in his earlier course not a whit behind either of the other two; Fletcher, later on, with his seraphic spirit, his powerful pen, and his fervent labour; the gradually widening circle of sympathetic clergymen and others who aided him in the work; and not least the itinerating "lay helpers," a noble band of men, toiling in heroic service, and often penetrating where the almost ubiquitous chief could not go ever ready to do his bidding, as he, with a general's skill, disposed them over the wide field of conflict; those of the lay preachers who were not set apart for the work, but who, as they were able, followed their trades and preached their sermons in their own neighbourhood, and hence were called "local preachers"; the needful leaders of the "classes" of believers, among whom were many godly, useful, and honoured women; the stewards who took charge of all financial affairs; and many others, each contributing according to his ability to the carrying on of the great campaign—all were welcomed, all were duly recognized and honoured, and even loved, for their work's sake.[16]

Wesley understood that humility is essential not just for leaders, but for all who long to be useful in the mission of God.

LEAD HUMBLY

My friend Mark Wilson leads like Wesley. We first met at a conference in California shortly after I had read an article about the rapid growth of the congregation he leads in the north woods of Wisconsin. Attendance at that church had increased from about fifty to more than five hundred people. And this remarkable growth happened in a town with a population of about two thousand. If that were my story, I might be a bit impressed with myself. Not Mark. He is modest and unassuming. We struck up an immediate friendship that continues to be a source of joy and encouragement. Mark went on to become a published author and speak to even larger crowds, but he never lost that common touch.

Mark finds his sense of self-worth in his relationship with God. He does not feel the need to impress anyone, so he is free to be who he is. He is the same person whether he just released another book or just released another fish from his line back into the Namekagon River. Because Mark is humble, people gladly follow him. He has attracted and maintained a strong team of leaders who have worked with him for more than twenty-five years.

When I think about my friend Mark, I am reminded of this quote from Andrew Murray, beloved South African author: "Humility is perfect quietness of heart. . . . It is to expect nothing, to wonder at nothing that is done to me, to feel nothing done against me. It is to be at rest when nobody praises me, and when I am blamed or despised."[17]

Of course, the person who is truly humble will be the first person to protest that he or she is not. Martin Luther is quoted as saying, "True humility does not know that it is humble. If it did, it would be proud from the contemplation of so fine a virtue."[18] In other words, true humility is an attainable but often elusive spiritual attribute. The conundrum is that the moment you feel that you have attained humility, it is lost. The apostle Paul's letter to the

Philippians frames the concept of humility in the context of the incarnation and ministry of Jesus:

> Therefore if you have any encouragement from being united with Christ, if any comfort from his love, if any common sharing in the Spirit, if any tenderness and compassion, then make my joy complete by being like-minded, having the same love, being one in spirit and of one mind. Do nothing out of selfish ambition or vain conceit. Rather, in humility value others above yourselves, not looking to your own interests but each of you to the interests of the others. In your relationships with one another, have the same mindset as Christ Jesus: Who, being in very nature God, did not consider equality with God something to be used to his own advantage; rather he made himself nothing by taking the very nature of a servant, being made in human likeness. And being found in appearance as a man, he humbled himself by becoming obedient to death—even death on a cross! (Phil. 2:1–8)

Find your sense of worth in the love of Christ not in the approval of others. The best way to develop humility is to keep your focus on loving God and serving others. To lead like Wesley is to lead humbly.

REFLECTION

1. Would those closest to me say I lead humbly?

2. How open am I to feedback and advice from those I lead?

3. Do I defend myself in matters that are unimportant for God's glory or the good of others? When was the last time I admitted that I was wrong about something?

4. When I am criticized, do I resent it or do I search for insight to help me lead more effectively?

7

LEAD
BOLDLY

Be fearless.

"Be ashamed of nothing but sin."

One of my favorite quotes from John Wesley is: "Give me one hundred preachers who fear nothing but sin and desire nothing but God, and I care not a straw whether they be clergymen or laymen, such alone will shake the gates of hell and set up the kingdom of heaven upon earth."[1] Notice that Wesley did not rely on ordained people alone to change the world. People who fear nothing but sin and desire nothing but God are those God will use. That is still true. God's team of world changers is not limited to a few people with academic degrees and clergy collars. God is looking for people who will boldly lead the only cause that counts for eternity.

For our purposes, boldness is defined as the courage to do the right thing, even in the face of opposition. This is not bravado but simple faith that takes the right action in spite of the cost. Boldness refuses to back down when the call to press forward is clear.

EXPECT CONFLICT

Volume 2 of Wesley's journals covers the middle years of his ministry, from December 1745 to May 1760. This one volume records at least thirty instances when Wesley and the early Methodists faced angry mobs. One of the more vivid examples comes from Wesley's ministry in Bolton in 1748:

> At one I went to the Cross in Bolton. There was a vast number of people, but many of them utterly wild. As soon as I began speaking, they began thrusting to and fro; endeavouring to throw me down from the steps on which I stood. They did so once or twice; but I went up again and continued my discourse. They then began to throw stones; at the same time some got up upon the Cross behind me to push me down; on which I could not but observe how God overrules even the minutest of circumstances. One man was bawling just at my ear, when a stone struck him on the cheek and he was still. A second was forcing his way down to me, till another stone hit him on the forehead: It bounded back, the blood ran down, and he came no farther. The third, being got close to me, stretched out his hand, and in the instant a sharp stone came upon the joints of his fingers. He shook his hand, and was very quiet till I concluded my discourse and went away.[2]

When preaching at Barnard-Castle a few years later, Wesley faced this experience: "The mob was so numerous and so loud, that it was not possible for many to hear. Nevertheless, I spoke on, and those who were near listened with huge attention. To prevent this, some of the rabble fetched the engine, and threw a good deal of water on the congregation; but not a drop fell on me. After about three quarters of an hour, I returned to the house."[3]

Persecution of this type was so frequent and intense that Wesley eventually made a practice of choosing preaching spots where the crowd did not have ready access to loose rocks or rotten vegetables.

Writing of his experience in Pocklington, Wesley described the process of selecting a site for his preaching: "I then looked at a yard which was proposed; but one circumstance of this I did not like. It was plentifully furnished with stones: Artillery ready at hand for the Devil's drunken companions."[4]

A few days later in Stokesley, Wesley learned that opposition to the Methodists was such that no one had yet succeeded in preaching in the public square. The most recent attempt, by Mr. Roberts, had been shut down by a large mob led by a member of the local clergy. Within an hour of Wesley's arrival, word began to spread through town, and news of a gathering mob made its way back to his host. When informed of their threats, Wesley was undaunted. He said, "Then there is no time to lose," and went out to preach. Later, he wrote, "I suppose the mob expected to hear us sing; but they were disappointed; for I began preaching without delay. By this means, missing their signal, they came, not in a body, but two or three at a time; and as fast as they came their minds were changed; so that all were quiet from beginning to the end."[5]

Catch the boldness of Wesley's reply: "Then there is no time to lose." He rushed in where others had been run off. Sometimes he preached on in spite of the mob. On one occasion, he rode to a town to preach precisely because he heard there might be a mob: "Being informed that some neighbouring gentlemen had declared they would apprehend the next preacher who came to Pensford, I rode over to give them a meeting: But none appeared."[6]

On another occasion, the Anglican priest in Shepton hired people to create a disturbance when Wesley came to town. The mob began throwing stones and clods of dirt on those who were trying to listen to Wesley. Wesley's journal entry reveals his approach to opposition:

"When I had done preaching, I would have gone out to them; it being my rule, confirmed by long experience, always to look a mob in the face."[7] That was John Wesley's preferred method of dealing with opposition: head-on.

Here is another of many examples that can be found in his journals: "I went on to Rood, where the mob threatened aloud. I determined however to look them in the face; and at twelve I cried, to the largest congregation by far which I had ever seen in these parts, 'Seek ye the Lord while he may be found; call ye upon him while he is near.' The despisers stood as men astonished, and neither spoke nor stirred till I had concluded my sermon."[8]

Four years later, after preaching in the city of Cork, Ireland, Wesley recorded this experience: "As soon as I came in to the street, the rabble threw whatever came to hand; but all went by me, or flew over my head; nor do I remember that one thing touched me. I walked on straight through the midst of the rabble, looking every man before me in the face; and they opened on the right and the left."[9]

On at least one occasion, Wesley identified the ringleader of a fierce mob and walked directly up to him with an outstretched hand. In a display of both surprise and courtesy, the ringleader responded to the unexpected gesture of friendship and became Wesley's defender for the rest of the evening. Here's the account in Wesley's own words:

After waiting about a quarter of an hour, perceiving the violence of the rabble still increasing, I walked down into the thickest of them and took the captain of the mob by the hand. He immediately said, "Sir, I will see you safe home. Sir, no man shall touch you. Gentlemen, stand off: Give back. I will knock the first man down that touches him." We walked on in great peace . . . till we came to Mr. Hide's door. We then parted in much love. I stayed in the street near half an hour after he was gone, talking with the people, who had now forgot their anger, and went away in high good humour.[10]

Wesley encountered opposition from politicians too, not just from mobs and jealous clergymen. After preaching to a mostly peaceful crowd in the small town of Shaftesbury on September 3, 1750, Wesley's evening meal was interrupted by the constable who proclaimed, "Sir, the Mayor discharges you from preaching in this borough any more." Wesley responded, "While King George gives me leave to preach, I shall not ask leave of the Mayor of Shaftesbury."[11]

Wesley knew his rights and, like the apostle Paul, was not reluctant to appeal to the highest civil authority (see Acts 25:10–12). Wesley was respectful but persistent in pressing his claim for religious freedom, as demonstrated in this excerpt from a letter to the mayor of Cork: "I fear God and honour the King. I earnestly desire to be at peace with all men: I have not willingly given any offence, either to the magistrates, the clergy, or any of the inhabitants of the city of Cork; neither do I desire anything of them, but to be treated (I will not say as a clergyman, a gentleman, or a Christian, but) with such justice and humanity as are due to a Jew, a Turk, or a pagan. I am, Sir, your obedient servant, John Wesley."[12]

One of the more violent encounters in Wesley's ministry occurred in Roughlee. While in the custody of a deputy constable, Richard Butler, Wesley was punched in the face. The captain of the military post there detained and later released Wesley. In his subsequent letter to the captain, Wesley stated his unrelenting commitment to fulfill his mission and his unwillingness to back down in the face of certain danger:

Soon after you and your friends came in, and required me to promise, I would come to Roughlee no more. I told you, I would sooner cut off my hand, than make any such promise. . . . And all this time you was [*sic*] talking of Justice and Law! Alas, Sir, suppose we were Dissenters (which I deny), suppose we were Jews or Turks, are we not to have the benefit of the laws of our country? Proceed against us by the law, if you can or dare; but not by lawless violence; not by making a drunken, cursing, swearing, riotous mob, both judge, jury, and executioner. This is flat rebellion against God and the King, as you may possibly find to your cost.[13]

Wesley was just as bold in dealing with problems within the church as in confronting opposition outside it. On one occasion when preaching in a church at Hayes, Wesley found the congregation well-mannered and attentive. Not so the choir. Wesley recorded his handling of the situation: "All behaved well but the singers, whom I reproved before the congregation; and some of them were ashamed."[14]

The Methodist society in Nottingham was floundering. Wesley arrived to assess the situation and did not take long to diagnose the problem or prescribe a solution: "I had long doubted what it was that hindered the work of God here. But upon inquiry the case was plain. So many of the society were triflers or disorderly walkers, that the blessing of God could not rest on them; so I made short work, cutting off all such at a stroke, and leaving only that little handful who (as far as could be judged) were really in earnest to save their souls."[15]

CONQUER SHAME WITH FORGIVENESS

One insight into Wesley's boldness comes from his journal record of an occasion when he failed to be bold with people who were not walking in truth. Writing about that failure, he confessed, "I felt a great damp, occasioned by my neglecting to speak plainly to some who were deceiving their own souls. I do not wonder at the last words of St. Augustine and Archbishop Usher, 'Lord, forgive me my sins of omission.'"[16] Wesley determined it was better to be bold before others than to stand ashamed before God someday, ashamed of what he had failed to do because of his fear of what others might think of him. Wesley observed this problem in his helpers also. Remarking on the shallow spirituality of the Methodist society in Swanage, he wrote, "I fear the preachers have been more studious to please than to awaken, or there would have been a deeper work."[17]

This desire to please others is a continual problem for leaders. When conducting seminars and conferences for leaders, I ask what they think is the main reason they aren't bolder for God. The most common responses center on the issue of fear: fear of failure, fear of rejection, fear of criticism.

The inhibiting effect of fear on leadership identified by Wesley is explored by Brené Brown in her book *Daring Greatly*. She quoted Peter Sheahan, CEO of ChangeLabs, on the undermining effect shame—which underlies our fear of rejection—has on our willingness to take bold risks: "The secret killer of innovation is shame. You can't measure it, but it is there. Every time someone holds back on a new idea, fails to give their manager much needed feedback, and is afraid to speak up in front of a client you can be sure shame played a part. That deep fear we all have of being wrong, of being belittled and of feeling less than, is what stops us taking the very risks required to move our companies forward. . . . Shame becomes fear. Fear leads to risk aversion. Risk aversion kills innovation."[18]

Brown argues that the essence of shame is the fear of disconnection, of not belonging and being loved. She contends that to escape from this shame, we must first understand what it is and acknowledge the grip it holds on us. To break shame's grip, Brown advises practicing vulnerability and valuing courage more than approval. As popular and helpful as Brown's book may be, there is a missing ingredient.

Based on the frequency with which John Wesley preached and taught from 1 John, it might be fair to say it was his favorite book of the Bible. In that epistle, the apostle John established the clear connection between being in fellowship with Christ and experiencing freedom from shame, resulting in courage. "And now, dear children, remain in fellowship with Christ so that when he returns, you will be full of courage and not shrink back from him in shame" (1 John 2:28 NLT).

As Christ-followers, we have a unique claim to boldness because of the grace and forgiveness we have experienced through faith in the sacrificial death our Lord Jesus. The writer to the Hebrews declared: "And so, dear brothers and sisters, we can boldly enter heaven's Most Holy Place because of the blood of Jesus. By his death, Jesus opened a new and life-giving way through the curtain into the Most Holy Place. And since we have a great High Priest who rules over God's house, let us go right into the presence of God with sincere hearts fully trusting him. For our guilty consciences have been sprinkled with Christ's blood to make us clean, and our bodies have been washed with pure water" (Heb. 10:19–22 NLT).

The person who has been forgiven and cleansed can be bold before God. Boldness before God overflows into boldness in human interactions. If God is for us, it doesn't matter who might be against us. "The wicked flee though no one pursues, but the righteous are as bold as a lion" (Prov. 28:1).

The leader who has first submitted to the lordship of Jesus Christ and experienced the cleansing and filling of the Holy Spirit is uniquely positioned to lead boldly in the mission of God. And boldness is essential to advancing the kingdom.

ATTRACT WITH CONFIDENCE

J. Oswald Sanders, author of *Spiritual Leadership*, wrote this to prospective leaders: "More failure comes from an excess of caution than from bold experiments with new ideas.... 'The frontiers of the kingdom of God were never advanced by men and women of caution.'"[19] Boldness is essential for capturing the heart of the next generation. Larry Alex Tauton's article on young atheists in *The Atlantic* states that many of these young people had arrived at their theological position after direct exposure to churches that were not living up to the dynamic potential of the gospel. "Serious-minded, they often concluded that church services were largely shallow, harmless, and ultimately irrelevant. As Ben, an engineering major at the University of Texas, so bluntly put it: 'I really started to get bored with church.'"[20]

Sherry and I have not been perfect parents, but we are blessed with four children who are vitally connected to Christ and his church. One of the things we purposely did when raising them was expose them to churches that were vibrant and focused on the mission. When I served as a district superintendent in West Michigan, our teenagers were blessed to be under the influence of passionate youth pastors like Jeff Eckart and Mark Carroll. These bold leaders challenged and inspired my children.

The church plants that we helped launch in Michigan became training grounds for our kids—John, Josiah, Joel, and Jordan—to serve and grow. Playing musical instruments on worship teams, joining in community service projects, and showing up early and staying late to help set up and then put away chairs—all of these opportunities allowed our kids to rub shoulders with people who were enthusiastic and fully engaged in the mission of God.

Our children had the privilege of assisting bold church planters like Chris Conrad, Mick Veach, Phil Struckmeyer, Chad McCallum, and Jon Allen. These leaders launched out in faith to create new congregations focused on bringing God glory, risking much to reach lost people with the good news of Jesus Christ. Boldness is inspiring.

Unfortunately, the bold leadership that produces dynamic churches is rare. Billy Graham's online daily devotional for June 8, 2015, shared this insight: "A great problem in America is that we have an anemic and watered-down Christianity that has produced an anemic, watered-down, and spineless Christian who is not willing to stand up and be counted on every issue. We must have a virile, dynamic, aggressive Christian who lives Christ seven days a week, who is ready to die, if necessary, for his [or her] faith. We need Christians who are ethical, honest, gracious, bold, strong, and devoted followers of the Lord Jesus Christ."[21] If our teams are going to be unashamed and bold, those of us who accept the challenge of leadership have to set the standard.

Before he was a missionary martyr, Jim Elliot was a young student in a Christian college wrestling with God's call on his life. He was looking for examples of bold leadership that he could emulate. One of the most convicting passages in all his writings comes in a journal entry made when he was just twenty-one years old, dated November 28, 1948:

Spent this afternoon with Ron. . . . They have a nice home and belongings and two cute kiddies, but are so like the rest of us that it is again disheartening. We are so utterly ordinary, so commonplace, while we profess to know a Power the twentieth century does not reckon with. But we are "harmless," and therefore unharmed. We are spiritual pacifists, non-militants, conscientious objectors in this battle-to-the-death with principalities and powers in high places. Meekness must be had for contact with men, but brass, outspoken boldness is required to take part in the comradeship of the cross. We are "sideliners"—coaching and criticizing the real wrestlers while content to sit by and leave the enemies of God unchallenged. The world cannot hate us, we are too much like its own. Oh that God would make us dangerous![22]

Jim Elliot took his own words seriously. He and his fellow missionaries pursued the dangerous goal of taking the gospel to an unreached people group among the Quechua people of Ecuador. Tragically, Elliot and four others lost their lives on the sandy shores of the Curaray River on January 8, 1952, at the hands of ten Huaorani warriors. But their deaths were not in vain. The boldness of their mission and their martyrdom was used by God to inspire and unleash a generation of missionaries who spread the gospel around the globe with renewed fervor.

Martin Luther provides another example of bold leadership. He experienced peace with God through faith and found freedom in the forgiveness of his sins. He was unashamed and would not back down before the opposition and threats levelled at him by the corrupt ecclesiastical bureaucracy.

Perhaps the most famous scene from his bold stand for the Reformation doctrines took place in the city of Worms before a religious tribunal in 1521. Among the many seated in judgment around Luther were the Holy Roman emperor, Charles; the governor, Frederick the Wise; and Eck, the archbishop of Trier. They held the power to banish or even execute Luther if found guilty of heresy.

The moment of truth came when the prosecutor challenged Luther, "Do you or do you not repudiate your books and the errors which they contain?" Luther boldly responded, "Since then Your Majesty and your lordships desire a simple reply, I will answer without horns and without teeth. Unless I am convicted by Scripture and plain reason—I do not accept the authority of popes and councils, for they have contradicted each other—my conscience is captive to the Word of God. I cannot and I will not recant anything, for to go against conscience is neither right nor safe. God help me. Amen. . . . . Here I stand, I cannot do otherwise."[23] Luther's boldness inspired thousands to join the Reformation, altering the course of Christian history.

LEAD BOLDLY

Wesley repeatedly faced opposition and persecution, including stonings, threats on his life, and being burned in effigy. Some Methodists were burned out of their homes and businesses. Others were beaten, one woman so severely that she miscarried. William Seward, a Methodist preacher, was struck by a rock while preaching the gospel in Wales. The blow knocked him unconscious, and he died from the wound a few days later, the first Methodist martyr.

You may never stand before an ecclesiastical tribunal or die as a missionary in a distant land, but there is always a price for leadership. If you are not experiencing any level of discomfort or opposition, you probably are not leading anything that makes a difference for the kingdom.

Author and business guru Seth Godin put it this way: "Leadership is scarce because few people are willing to go through the discomfort required to lead. . . . It's uncomfortable to propose an idea that might fail. It's uncomfortable to challenge the status quo. It's uncomfortable to resist the urge to settle. When you identify the discomfort, you've found the place where a leader is needed. If you're not uncomfortable in your work as a leader, it's almost certain you're not reaching your potential as a leader."[24] If that's true for people simply trying to lead a business, how much more true will it be for those leading the greatest cause of all?

One of the finest examples of this boldness I have witnessed firsthand was the courage of Rev. Dr. Richard Waugh, national superintendent of The Wesleyan Methodist Church of New Zealand and pastor of East City Wesleyan Church in Auckland. Prior to that, Waugh was one of the more successful and respected pastors in a large mainline denomination in that country. As an evangelical with full confidence in the authority of Scripture, he stood as a minority voice against the liberal and compromising majority that controlled that denomination. Finally, after exhausting all possible means of calling that ecclesiastical body to return to its godly heritage, Waugh and a few other faithful leaders stepped out to launch a new evangelical church-planting Methodist body.

I had the privilege of working alongside Waugh and other members of this fledgling organization for several years in the areas of leadership development and church planting. I heard their stories and learned about the personal sacrifices they had made to take this stand of conscience. A flourishing Christian movement exists in New Zealand today because this team was willing to lead boldly.

To make a difference in our generation, we must step up, take risks, and lead boldly. Courage fueled by faith is essential, not optional, for leaders. "Therefore, since we have such a hope, we are very bold" (2 Cor. 3:12). Be ashamed of nothing but sin. Work hard and stay humble. You may not encounter the same opposition faced by John Wesley, but leadership is never for the timid. To lead like Wesley is to lead boldly.

REFLECTION

1. What is the biggest leadership risk I have taken recently?

2. In which of my leadership responsibilities do I most need boldness?

3. What big risk could God be calling our team or organization to take in the near future?

4. What might be keeping me from leading more boldly? Is there anything in my life that causes me to be ashamed?

8

LEAD
CONSISTENTLY

Keep your commitments.

"Be punctual. Do everything exactly at the time."

At first glance, rule 8 appears to be a restatement of Wesley's first rule on diligence. However, this rule on punctuality extends the principle of diligence from self-discipline into social relationships and leadership obligations. Remember that Wesley's goal was to instill behavior that would advance the movement. He was mobilizing a team of leaders in an era when mass communication was limited to the printing press. Wesley's advice to his lay preachers was vital then and is still a useful reminder for leaders today: "Be sure never to disappoint a congregation, unless in case of life or death. Begin and end precisely at the time appointed."[1]

Credibility is a critical element for all leaders, especially those building a movement in its early stages. That was certainly true for the Methodists. Punctuality was then, and is now, a practical behavior that builds credibility. If Wesley said he was going to appear in the public square at Devonshire to preach at noon, he had to be there at noon. If he said he would preach to the coal miners at five o'clock before they went to work, arriving thirty minutes late was not an option. It was essential to begin on time. It was just as important to end on time. If the workers arrived late for work because they were caught up in the early morning sermon, they would give Methodism a bad reputation and might even lose their jobs.

Wesley went to great lengths to keep his commitments. His punctuality, self-discipline, and consistent ministry practices produced a movement that endured long after his death. Wesley led consistently.

BE PUNCTUAL

On one occasion, someone announced that Wesley would preach in the town of Stanley, even though Wesley himself had not made that commitment. Nevertheless, he knew what he had to do: "I designed to have rested on Wednesday, but finding that notice had been given of my preaching at Stanley, we got thither, through roads almost impassable, about noon, and found more people than the house could contain; so I stood in the yard, and proclaimed free salvation to a loving, simple people. Several were in tears and all of them so thankful that I could not repent of my labour."[2]

Wesley and his followers were called Methodists because of their consistent practice of spiritual disciplines. They fasted on Tuesdays and Fridays, and the time usually given to meal preparation and consumption was offered to God in prayer. The money that would have purchased food was given to the poor.

Wesley believed that inconsistency showed a lack of spiritual and organizational health. He was also convinced that inconsistency was a cause of spiritual ill health, not just an effect. Where members of Methodist societies were faithful in attending their weekly class and band meetings, both the individuals and the society as a whole prospered. Where people were haphazard in meeting at the appointed time, they declined spiritually and the Methodist society suffered.

Punctuality is a statement of mutual respect. If we have all agreed to meet at a designated time, there is an obligation, especially for the leader, to honor that commitment. Unless there is a clear impediment such as a traffic accident or delayed airline flight, failing to appear punctually communicates a lack of value for another's time. It may also indicate a lack of self-discipline.

The leader who cannot manage him- or herself well enough to ensure a timely arrival should not be surprised to find people following that example. A team that has to cope with rampant inconsistency, even in minor considerations, will find itself dealing with larger problems of trust over time.

To maintain the value for punctuality in the movement, Wesley knew his helpers needed to develop consistency in their private lives. Personal discipline spills over into our public lives. Others have noted the connection between seemingly small habits and success in life. Will Durant, paraphrasing Aristotle's wisdom, wrote, "We are what we repeatedly do. Excellence, then, is not an act, but a habit."[3] John Dryden put it this way: "We first make our habits, and then our habits make us."[4]

Wesley was asked at one of the annual conferences, "Do we sufficiently watch over our helpers?" He responded with a list of questions that were to be asked frequently of those assisting in leadership of the movement:

- Do you walk closely with God?
- Have you now fellowship with the Father and the Son?
- At what hour do you rise?

- Do you punctually observe the morning and evening hour of retirement?
- Do you spend the day in the manner which we advise?
- Do you converse seriously, usefully, and closely?
- To be more particular: Do you use all the means of grace yourself, and enforce the use of them on all other persons?[5]

Some of these questions are exactly what you would expect for leaders in a ministry organization. Others might surprise you. When was the last time your supervisor asked you what time you got out of bed this morning? Wesley realized that being on time for a morning appointment actually begins the night before—with going to bed early enough to get sufficient sleep to get up on time so you can be punctual. Wesley believed that punctuality originated in good habits. He was convinced that these habits would, over time, shape the leader's character.

BE ACCURATE AND PRECISE

Punctuality, as the word was used in Wesley's day, included the idea of being exact or precise. The need for consistency stretched beyond arriving at the time for scheduled meetings. Wesley viewed punctuality as including accuracy in statistical reporting and record keeping:

I inquired into the state of the society [in Dublin]. Most pompous accounts had been sent me, from time to time, of the great numbers that were added to it; so that I could confidently expect to find therein six or seven hundred members. And how is the real fact? I left three hundred and [*sic*] ninety-four members; and I doubt if there are now three hundred and [*sic*] ninety-six!

Let this be a warning to us all, how we give in to that hateful custom of painting things beyond the life. Let us make a conscience of magnifying or exaggerating any thing. Let us rather speak under, than above, the truth. We, of all men, should be punctual in all we say; that none of our words may fall to the ground.[6]

Wesley was exactly right. To become leaders that people willingly follow, we owe it to them to "be punctual in all we say." Rounding up when estimating attendance at an event and rounding off when announcing the start time ("five-ish," as some say) is the opposite of punctuality. Those we lead have every right to expect that our words and actions will be correct and consistent.

After determining that a board of twelve trustees was too large to effectively manage the business affairs of a Methodist society, Wesley reduced the number to seven. When he announced the change, he also updated the instructions for their meetings and included the following charge: "The chairman is to see, that all the rules be punctually observed, and immediately check him who breaks any of them."[7] Wesley expected nothing less than consistency, "that all the rules be punctually observed." Punctuality was the leader's obligation to the team.

After Wesley conducted a quarterly meeting with Methodist society stewards in Ireland, he entered this note in his journal: "Nothing is wanting in this kingdom but zealous, active preachers, tenacious of order and exact discipline."[8]

BE CONSISTENT

It is not surprising that many ecclesiastical bodies that find their roots in the soil of Methodism call their handbook *The Discipline.*

Wesley advocated for passionate leadership but understood that without consistency, much of the fruit of their labors would be lost. Wesley learned the value of punctuality at home and practiced it throughout his life. From the early years of disciplined training under his mother's tutelage to his days with the Holy Club at Oxford University, Wesley practiced rigorous self-discipline in his personal and public life.

On Wesley's seventy-second birthday, June 28, 1774, he reflected on his good health. He found himself to be as strong as he had been thirty years earlier. He gave the credit to God for this but also described some of the consistent practices he believed God blessed: "The chief means are, 1. My constantly rising at four, for about fifty years. 2. My generally preaching at five in the morning; one of the most healthy exercises in the world. 3. My never traveling less, by sea or land, than four thousand five hundred miles in a year."[9]

Field preaching, publicly declaring God's grace and kingdom in the open air, was Wesley's prime strategy for awakening people to their sin and calling them to a life of holiness. This public proclamation brought Methodism to the attention of the common folk in England. Wesley was questioned whether it might be possible that the Methodists used open-air preaching too infrequently. He responded with the following:

It seems we have; (1) Because our call is, to save that which is lost. Now, we cannot expect them to seek us. Therefore we should go and seek them. (2) Because we are particularly called, by "going into the highways and hedges," which none else will do, "to compel them to come in." (3) Because that reason against it is not good, "The house will hold all that come." The house may hold all that come to the house; but not all that would come to the field.

The greatest hindrance to this you are to expect from rich, or cowardly, or lazy Methodists. But regard them not, neither stewards, leaders, nor people. Whenever the weather will permit, go out in God's name into the most public places, and call all to repent and believe the gospel; every Sunday, in particular; especially were [*sic*] there are old societies, lest they settle upon their lees.[10]

Wesley encouraged consistency in this practice and warned that opposition to it would come primarily from within the organization, from those who were too timid or had grown complacent. He was concerned that failing to consistently employ this effective practice would mark the beginning of the decline of the Methodist movement. Reflecting on the lukewarm spiritual climate of the society in Whitehaven, Wesley concluded, "The want of field-preaching has been one cause of deadness here. I do not find any great increase of the work of God without it. If ever this is laid aside, I expect the whole work will gradually die away."[11]

Wesley was consistent in his methods and in his message. One critic accused Wesley of changing his doctrine of Christian perfection through the years. Wesley responded, "I dislike the saying, this was not known or taught among us till within two or three years. I grant that you did not know it. You have over and over denied instantaneous sanctification to me; but I have known and taught it (and so has my brother, as our writings show) above these twenty years."[12] Wesley's message of justification by faith, assurance of peace with God through the witness of the Holy Spirit, and the possibility of having a heart sanctified or fully devoted to God, were the building blocks of the movement.

Do not mistake Wesley's consistency with aversion to change. While not all changes result in improvement, all improvements require change. The wise leader understands that the mission never changes but the methods must change constantly. Good leaders prepare the organization to expect continual changes of method. Wesley wrote, "I would observe every punctilio of order, except where the salvation of souls is at stake. There I prefer the end before the means."[13]

Wesley was so open to experimentation that some of his critics attacked his constant innovation, what they labeled as "this changing one thing after another continually." He responded, "That with regard to these little prudential helps we are continually changing one thing after another, is not a weakness or fault, as you imagine, but a peculiar advantage which we enjoy. By this means we declare them all to be merely prudential, not essential, not of divine institution. . . . We are always open to instruction; willing to be wiser every day than we were before, and to change whatever we can change for the better."[14]

"Methods are many, principles are few. Methods always change, principles never do."[15] Like many of the leadership maxims that I have collected through the years, I believe I first heard this from my youth ministry mentor, Keith Drury. Others give credit to Warren Wiersbe.

Although Wesley recognized the need to ensure that methods evolved to suit the demands of the hour, he faithfully adhered to scriptural principles: "In religion, I am for as few innovations as possible. I love the old wine best."[16]

GENERATE TRUST

Laszlo Bock, senior vice president of people operations at Google, shared the following insights from Google's big data research on best leadership practices in an interview with *The New York Times*: "We found that, for leaders, it's important that people know you are consistent and fair in how you think about making decisions and that there's an element of predictability. If a leader is consistent, people on their teams experience tremendous freedom, because then they know that within certain parameters, they can do whatever they want. If your manager is all over the place, you're never going to know what you can do, and you're going to experience it as very restrictive."[17] Did you catch that? "If a leader is consistent, people on their teams experience tremendous freedom."

Mr. Grimshaw provided a positive example of the freedom team members can experience under consistent leadership. He served as a deacon in the Church of England and joined the Methodists in Hawthorn for twenty years, until his death in 1762. Wesley recalled that Grimshaw would not "rest satisfied without taking every method he thought likely to spread the knowledge of his God and Saviour. And as the very indigent constantly made their want of better clothes to appear in, an excuse for not going to church in the day-time, he contrived, for them chiefly, a lecture on Sunday evenings; though he had preached twice the day before. God was pleased to give great success to these attempts, which animated him still more to spend and be spent for Christ."[18]

Predictability matters today. It mattered even more in Wesley's day. If people expected him to preach in their town at five the next morning, they made the effort to be there. If he didn't show up or arrived late, they would be less likely to come out the next time. If we say the meeting will begin at seven and end by eight thirty, we create an expectation. If we show up late and keep people past the time for adjournment, they will not burn us at the stake but we will lose credibility. No leader can meet all expectations, but good leaders *always* meet the expectations they set.

Wesley knew that consistency would build confidence, and confidence would build momentum. He also knew that the opposite was true. If inconsistency crept into his practice and that of his leaders, others would lose confidence in them. If confidence eroded, momentum would stall, and the movement would falter. Consistency matters even in small things such as punctuality. Laurel Buckingham, my mentor and friend, often reminds his students that there are four keys to success:

1. Show up on time.
2. Do what you say you're going to do.
3. Finish what you start.
4. Say please and thank you.

Over a lifetime of leadership experience, Buckingham observed that successful leaders consistently practice those four rules. He also saw that ineffective leaders consistently violated one or more of those rules. Leading consistently, even in what might seem to be small matters, reveals the leader's respect for others and seriousness about the assignment.

In Jesus' parable of the talents, the master offered this commendation to the two servants who doubled their investment: "Well done, good and faithful servant! You have been faithful with a few things; I will put you in charge of many things" (Matt. 25:21). Paul instructed Timothy to be selective in choosing whom to entrust with the gospel message and ministry: "And the things you have heard me say in the presence of many witnesses entrust to reliable people who will also be qualified to teach others" (2 Tim. 2:2).

If you cannot be a good steward of your time or the time of others, why should you be entrusted with matters of eternal significance? If consistency matters even in small things, it is even more important in the larger commitment to the mission. W. Edwards Deming, father of quality management, is said to have insisted, "There must be consistency in direction."[19]

In his book *Good to Great*, Jim Collins proposed the leadership concept of the flywheel. He discovered that organizations that moved off the plateau of mediocrity to breakout levels of success were not overnight sensations. They had done the right things consistently for years. Once the compass was set, the most successful organizations kept on a steady course with determined resolve. "No matter how dramatic the end result, the good-to-great transformations never happened in one fell swoop. There was no single defining action, no grand program, no one killer innovation, no solitary lucky break, no miracle moment. Rather, the process resembled relentlessly pushing a giant heavy flywheel in one direction, turn upon turn, building momentum until a point of breakthrough, and beyond."[20]

John Symonds answered a call to pastoral ministry later in life after a career as a high school teacher. Symonds completed his ministerial training at Asbury Theological Seminary and then returned to his home region to lead a church in Yarmouth, Nova Scotia. The church was not thriving when he arrived, but Symonds was determined to make a difference. He immediately instituted a home visitation initiative, announcing to the congregation that every Tuesday evening he would visit in the homes of recent church guests or others from the congregation.

The church did not turn around in a few weeks or even months, but over time, Symonds's consistent practice began to pay off. The church grew from fifty to seventy to one hundred twenty to two hundred to three hundred to four hundred and eventually became the largest evangelical church in that region. Hundreds of lives were transformed for eternity as the church flourished under his leadership.

What would have happened if Symonds made these visits on some Tuesday nights and not others? Imagine how you might feel if you showed up on a Tuesday evening to join him for visitation only to learn that he had cancelled at the last minute to attend a hockey game. You might conclude that he was not all that committed. And if the leader is not that committed, no one else will be.

What might have happened if Symonds started the practice of home visitation for a few months but then gave it up to launch a different program? And what if the new program was shelved a month or two later in favor of a third initiative? I suspect the people on his team would grow less than enthusiastic with the launch of each new program.

Never underestimate the value of consistency. Doing the right things over time produces results. The compounding effect works in investing, and it works in leadership too. This is not a call for stubborn or dogmatic use of methods that have been proven ineffective. If the horse is dead, don't buy a longer whip or sharper spurs. But when you do find principles that are enduring, consistently practice them.

Pete Benson, a childhood friend of mine and the founder of a respected investment firm, kept on practicing the financial disciplines he first learned as a struggling college student. He continued those practices long after he graduated and began working for a nonprofit organization. Early on, Pete determined never to borrow money for a depreciating asset, so he would buy a car only if he could afford to pay for it in cash. He would drive that car as long as he could while saving money to pay cash for the next one. In those early days, Pete drove older, clunky vehicles while many of his friends drove brand-new cars, which they'd borrowed money to obtain. Pete stuck to his plan and has followed that practice consistently for thirty years. Some of his friends laughed at him in the beginning, but they don't laugh now. Today, he can afford to pay cash for finer vehicles than most of his friends can buy on credit. Pete can do what he does today because for many years he did what others were unwilling to do.

LEAD CONSISTENTLY

To be punctual, you plan ahead and allow margin. The unexpected will happen, often when you have the least capacity to respond. So leave early to arrive on time. My father was fond of reminding me that "it's better to be five minutes early than one minute late."

Consistent punctuality communicates reliability. When you show yourself to be reliable long enough, your scope of authority will increase. Little things add up. Spend less. Save more. Eat less. Exercise more. Promise less. Deliver more. Do these simple things consistently over time and you will eventually reap compounding rewards. You will build greater self-confidence, and you will earn the confidence of others.

Wesley modeled exactly what he preached in this regard, though it wasn't always easy to do. Year after year he rode across the hills and valleys of the British Isles, proclaiming the good news of full salvation in Christ. As mentioned before, one of the consistent methods Wesley employed was preaching at five each morning: "To this day field-preaching is a cross to me. But I know my commission, and see no other way of 'preaching the gospel to every creature.'"[21]

Wesley continued this consistent practice into his late eighties, punctually preaching in the fields before sunrise until just a few months before his death in March 1791. And what was the result? One author observed that when Wesley was carried to his grave, he left behind "a good library of books, a well-worn clergyman's gown . . . and the Methodist Church."[22] The return on his consistent investment was most notably evidenced in the 135,000 Methodist society members and 541 itinerant preachers who remained to carry on his great work.

If you want to lead like Wesley, lead consistently.

REFLECTION

1. Do I build confidence in others and momentum in my organization by leading consistently?

2. Is that as true in small things as in the larger matters of my leadership?

3. What one habit or skill, if consistently practiced over the next few years, would have a significant impact on my leadership?

4. How will I build margin into my life so I can be punctual in delivering on the things that matter most?

9

LEAD
ACCOUNTABLY

Submit to the authority of others.

*"Do not mend our Rules, but keep them; not for wrath,
but for conscience' sake."*

Wesley understood that he would give a strict account to God for his words, time, money, and energy. He knew that his life was not his own. He often spoke of God's providence in his rescue from a house fire on February 9, 1709, when he was just five years old. That night Wesley's father quoted an Old Testament Scripture that spoke of a "burning stick snatched from the fire" (Zech. 3:2; Amos 4:11). Wesley knew that he had to make his life count.

The reason we have Wesley's journals and letters is that he was challenged, as a young Oxford student, to give an account for every hour: "It was in pursuance of an advice given by Bishop Taylor, in his 'Rules for Holy Living and Dying,' that, about fifteen years ago, I began to take a more exact account than I had done before, of the manner wherein I spent my time, writing down how I had employed every hour."[1]

Wesley understood and embraced the accountability he owed to God, and the principle of accountability runs through the rules we have already considered. In this ninth rule, Wesley expanded the scope of accountability and called leaders to embrace mutual accountability with the community within which they lived and served.

LEADERS ARE ACCOUNTABLE FOR THEIR WORK

From his early days with the Holy Club at Oxford, Wesley carried a sense of shared stewardship. He and other members of the group were criticized for their strict observance of fasting, even though they used the money saved on buying food to provide charity to prisoners. Wesley wrote to his father seeking counsel. Toward the conclusion of their correspondence, Wesley included these few lines which are an early expression of his understanding of accountability: "And in the resolution to adhere to these and all things else which we are convinced God requires at our hands, we trust we shall persevere till he calls us to give an account of our stewardship." Later, while aboard a ship en route to his ministry appointment in Georgia, Wesley continued the practice of group accountability: "At twelve we met to give an account to one another what we had done since our last meeting, and what we designed to do before our next."[2]

While the Methodist movement was still very young, Wesley appointed individuals to visit members of the society who were sick and confined to their homes. He gave written instructions to the first dozen he appointed, recorded in this journal entry from May 7, 1741: "Visit and provide things needful for the sick. Each of these is to visit all the sick within their district, every other day: And to meet on Tuesday evening, to give an account of what they have done, and consult what can be done farther."[3] Those entrusted with responsibility and authority to act were also responsible to give an account of their actions to the team. Then they were to consult together about the appropriate next steps.

In his journal entry of June 4, 1751, Wesley provided even more specific guidelines to those entrusted with the care of Methodist properties and finances. Among the eleven rules was this clear direction to the chairperson: "You are to take it in turn, month by month, to be Chairman. The Chairman is to see, that all the rules be punctually observed, and immediately to check him who breaks any of them."[4] These rules for stewards were to be closely followed. Any steward who broke the rules three times, if admonished by the chair and noted in the minutes, would forfeit the right to continue in that office.

Wesley did not create rules simply to prove he was in charge. He was also acting as steward of the movement. He did not call for blind obedience and gladly took time to explain the rationale behind the rules: "I purposely delayed examining the classes, till I had gone through the Rules of the Society, part of which I explained to them at large, with the reasons of them, every morning."[5]

Wesley's own pattern of consulting with and being accountable to his brother and other members of the Holy Club became institutionalized in the Methodist practice as the conference. During conferences, Wesley met with a society to hear reports of their progress, answer questions about Methodist doctrine or practice, and ensure the accountability of leaders and members to one another and the movement. Conferences came to be held annually, although Wesley was not reluctant to call them more often if he determined that would be helpful. Wesley deeply valued these times of conferencing. He really did long to be part of a band of brothers committed to one another and committed together to this great cause:

Our conference began; and the more we conversed, the more brotherly love increased. The same spirit we found on Tuesday and Wednesday. I expected to have heard many objections to our first doctrines; but none appeared to have any: We seemed to be all of one mind, as well as one heart. . . .

I mentioned whatever I thought was amiss, or wanting, in any of our brethren. It was received in a right spirit, with much love, and serious, earnest attention; and, I trust, not one went from the conference discontented; but rather, blessing God for the consolation.[6]

CREATE A SHARED STANDARD

Wesley poured his life into the Methodist movement. His best energy and all his personal financial resources were surrendered to this mission. He traveled extensively, sometimes riding as long as twenty hours at a stretch. He worked tirelessly, preaching up to five times in a day. When in a town for more than a day, he took time to interview every single member of each society assigned to his care. It is not surprising, then, that he had high expectations for his team members. He never asked anyone to do more than he himself was willing to do. Those who joined his team did so voluntarily. They raised their hand and asked to help him in this grand endeavor:

> These severally desired to serve me as sons, and to labour when and where I should direct. Observe: These likewise desired me, not I them. But I durst not refuse their assistance. And here commenced my power, to appoint each of these when, and where, and how to labour; that is, while he chose to continue with me. For each had a power to go away when he pleased; as I had also, to go away from them, or any of them, if I saw sufficient cause.

The case continued the same when the number of preachers increased. I had just the same power still, to appoint when, and where, and how each should help me; and to tell any (if I saw cause), "I do not desire your help any longer." On these terms, and no other, we joined at first: On these we continue joined. But they do me no favour in being directed by me. It is true, my "reward is with the Lord": But at present I have nothing from it but trouble and care; and often a burden I scarce know how to bear. . . .

Every preacher and every member may leave me when he pleases. But while he chooses to stay, it is on the same terms that he joined me at first.[7]

Wesley never surrendered the power to appoint workers to their respective assignments. He believed that, since these men and women had volunteered to assist him, they would do so under the terms first established for as long as he and they were both willing to continue that relationship. They were assisting him. He did not pursue them, and they were not legally obligated to him. If they were willing to assist, that was well and good; however, they would do so on his terms or not at all.

Many of Wesley's helpers faithfully fulfilled their assignments, but others were significant disappointments. Imagine how Wesley must have felt to arrive at Epworth, his hometown, only to discover the declining state of the Methodist society there: "We returned to Epworth, to a poor, dead, senseless people: At which I did not wonder, when I was informed, 1. That some of our preachers there had diligently gleaned up and retailed all the evil they could hear of me: 2. That some of them had quite laid aside our hymns, as well as the doctrine they formerly preached: 3. That one of them had frequently spoke against our Rules, and the others quite neglected them. Nothing, therefore, but the mighty power of God could have kept the people so well as they were."[8]

Wesley had enough critics and opponents outside the Methodist movement. Little wonder that he was disappointed, even frustrated, when his own team members undermined the very movement they had promised to nurture and protect.

Adhering to mutually agreed upon expectations was the glue of the Methodist movement. To provide guidance to a fast-growing enterprise without the speed of electronic communication that we take for granted today was a nearly impossible task. Accountability to standards of practice was vital.

Wesley welcomed the assistance of any who chose to align themselves with him but rightfully expected that they would embrace his sense of accountability for conduct. He empowered leaders to operate with great freedom within their appointments. Yet he insisted that they follow the clear guidelines he provided and remain diligent in performing their duties: "Remember! A Methodist preacher is to mind every point, great and small, in the Methodist discipline! Therefore you will need all the sense you have, and to have all your wits about you! . . . Act in all things, not according to your own will, but as a son in the gospel. . . . Above all, if you labour with us in our Lord's vineyard, it is needful you should do that part of the work which we advise, at those times and places which we judge most for his glory."[9]

Solon, the Greek philosopher-statesman (638–558 BC), is credited as being the first to say, "Learn to obey before you command."[10] Wesley learned obedience at home under the strict tutelage of his mother, Susanna Wesley. Submitting to authority was a constant theme for Wesley. He held obedience as evidence of true faith. He critiqued even the American revolutionaries for their rebellion against the duly constituted authority they had pledged to obey.

Wesley asked Methodist society members to submit to the leaders he had appointed over them. He expected, at the least, that these leaders would operate within the guidelines he had established.

Interdependence was Wesley's ideal. Independence was the reality he too often encountered, as in this case, noted in his journal one Easter day: "I preached at seven, on, 'The Lord is risen indeed,' with an uncommon degree of freedom; and then met the local preachers, several of whom seemed to have caught the fashionable disease—desire of independency. They were at first very warm; but at length agreed to act by the Rules laid down in the minutes of the conference."[11]

Independence from authority was fashionable then, and its appeal continues today. To be clear, Wesley was not opposed to people taking initiative. He took exception to those who professed loyalty in order to be entrusted with authority but then acted contrary to the ways agreed upon when Wesley rode out of town.

REQUIRE ACCOUNTABILITY FROM OTHERS

Wesley was convinced that faithfully applying the practices that had birthed the movement was vital to its continued growth. When he returned to Aberdeen, Scotland, in May 1784, Wesley found that the bands and select society had continued meeting but that their spiritual passion was low. He diagnosed the problem and urged his leadership team to remedy the situation:

Many were faint and weak for want of morning preaching and prayer-meetings, of which I found scant traces in Scotland. In the evening I talked largely with the preachers, and showed them the hurt it did both to them and the people, for any one preacher to stay six or eight weeks together in one place. Neither can he find matter for preaching every morning and evening, nor will the people come to hear him. Hence he grows cold by lying in bed, and so do the people. Whereas, if he never stays more than a fortnight together in one place, he may find matter enough, and the people will gladly hear him. They immediately drew up such a plan for this circuit, which they determined to pursue.[12]

Wesley's insistence on itinerant ministry allowed the people to hear fresh voices proclaiming the same message. Some of the circuit riders found a responsive audience and comfortable accommodations tempting. Why ride on to a town that might be less welcoming? Yet Wesley knew that many of the ministers were limited to preaching from the basic outlines that he provided. He suspected that after a few weeks, they could not help but repeat themselves. That would be boring for them and detrimental for their audience. A dull sermon is hard enough to endure at eleven in the morning. Imagine trying to listen to one at five! So the infrequent rotation of itinerant preachers caused morning attendance to decline and services to be cancelled.

Yet morning preaching was vital to the movement. It not only sent the Methodists off to work with fresh inspiration, but also set the tone for the rest of the leader's day. Wesley was convinced that drowsy preachers could not lead thriving teams.

Notice in this case that Wesley made the case for action, but it was the team that "immediately drew up" the plan. Accountability, properly understood and embraced, is energizing. Michael Hyatt, former CEO of Thomas Nelson and a prolific blogger, made this point: "Everyone wants to be a leader. However, few are prepared to accept the accountability that goes with it. But you can't have one without the other. They are two sides of the same coin."[13]

Patrick Lencioni tackled the issue of accountability head-on in his *New York Times* best-selling book *The Five Dysfunctions of a Team*. His consulting firm, The Table Group, provided an online survey based on Lencioni's model that allowed members to evaluate their team's function. Nearly fifteen thousand assessments were tabulated by 2006 with the following results: Among the highest scores for dysfunction on these teams were: avoidance of commitment (25 percent), inattention to results (28 percent), fear of conflict (39 percent), and absence of trust (44 percent). Outstripping all those factors as the most frequent dysfunction in teams was this lone factor: lack of accountability (68 percent).

And that assessment included not just the bottom tier of the organization. Lencioni's assessment revealed that lack of accountability was more likely to be a fundamental concern higher up in the organization. The study of 132 executive teams found that 80 percent self-reported as not providing adequate accountability for behaviors and results.[14]

The Table Group's research on teamwork continued with more than twenty thousand surveys completed by 2012. Lack of accountability continued to be the number one concern. In response to this ongoing problem, Lencioni commented:

> Accountability is absolutely essential in developing a high performing team. Teams that are behaviorally and intellectually aligned, have constructive conflict, and make firm commitments need to have the ability to push each other to stick to those commitments in the spirit of achieving results. When teams suffer from a breakdown in accountability, results do suffer.
>
> For teams that have never engaged in this direct form of feedback, it may seem harsh. In reality, it is quite the opposite. To hold a team member accountable for his/her actions shows that person you actually care about them enough to take the interpersonal risk to discuss the issue. When feedback is given according to the outlined agreements, it can help a team member's personal/professional development and the progress of the team.[15]

Joseph Grenny and his researchers found a marked difference between weak and strong teams in their practice of accountability. Weak teams have no accountability, mediocre teams default to the boss as the source of accountability, and high-performing teams diligently hold one another accountable.[16]

Wesley understood that accountability was vital to the Methodist movement. If he was to entrust leadership authority to as many as five hundred team members branching out across England, Ireland, Scotland, and, eventually, the United States, he would have to ensure that there was accountability to his clear instructions.

The rules and the conference were essential tools for ensuring this. The rules provided the playbook by which the circuit riders, stewards, and society leaders were to operate. The conference provided an ongoing opportunity for feedback and accountability.

These conferences included question-and-answer sessions with Wesley, during which he could clarify practice and doctrine and receive reports from team members. In these intimate settings, Wesley provided feedback to his team. The following journal entries reveal how it worked:

I mentioned whatever I thought was amiss, or wanting, in any of our brethren. It was received in a right spirit, with much love, and serious, earnest attention; and, I trust, not one went from the conference discontented; but rather, blessing God for the consolation. . . .

We had a little conference with about thirty preachers. I particularly inquired concerning their grace, and gifts, and fruit; and found reason to doubt of one only. . . .

Most of our preachers met, and conversed freely together; as we did, morning and afternoon, to the end of the week; when our conference ended with the same blessing as it began: God giving us all to be not only of one heart, but of one judgment.[17]

Wesley wanted a forum to ensure the helpers' accountability to him, but he also sought their counsel and guidance for leading the movement: "I desired Mr. Fletcher, Dr. Coke, and four more of our brethren to meet every evening, that we might consult together on any difficulty that occurred. On Tuesday our conference began, at which were present about seventy preachers whom I had severally invited to come and assist me with their advice, in carrying on the great work of God."[18]

Wesley wanted people not only to comply with the rules, but also to understand the rationale behind them. He made himself accountable to the group members and practiced full disclosure: "I began reading and explaining to the society, the large minutes of the conference. I desire to do all things openly and above-board. I would have all the world, and especially all of our society, see not only all the steps we take, but the reasons why we take them."[19]

SUBMIT TO ACCOUNTABILITY

One of John Wesley's more controversial expectations was that his leaders not consider marriage without first consulting other leaders in the movement. This was one of the original twelve rules of a helper. Wesley believed that, even in this most personal concern, a decision should not be made without consulting one's peers. He said, "Let all be exhorted to take no step in so weighty a matter without advising with the most serious of their brethren. . . . Take no step toward marriage, without first consulting with your brethren."[20]

Wesley followed this rule himself. He was still a bachelor at the age of forty-six when he fell in love with Grace Murray. Wesley submitted the possibility of a marriage to his brother Charles, who immediately expressed disapproval. He counseled John against this marriage and then, to close the door completely, Charles met privately with Grace Murray and strongly urged her to marry another man, which she did.

John was heartbroken. It is no wonder that the next time he considered marriage he did not seek Charles's advice. This time he consulted other trusted advisors, including Mr. Perronet. "Having received a full answer from Mr. P——, I was clearly convinced that I ought to marry. For many years I remained single, because I believed I could be more useful in a single, than in a married state. And I praise God, who enabled me so to do. I now as fully believed, that in my present circumstances, I might be more useful in a married state; into which, upon this clear conviction, and by the advice of my friends, I entered a few days after."[21]

Unfortunately, Wesley's marriage to Mrs. Veazel, a wealthy widow, did not turn out as he hoped. He refused to limit the rigorous schedule of his itinerant ministry, and she could not endure the pace and discomforts to which Wesley had become so accustomed. Eventually she came to resent both his frequent travels and his continued written correspondence with many women who were friends in the Methodist movement.

The matter came to a sad conclusion. On January 23, 1771, Mrs. Wesley abandoned her husband in London. He records only a brief journal entry that day, explaining that she "set out for Newcastle, purposing 'never to return.' *Non eam reliqui: Non dimisi: Non revocabo.*" The publisher of the 1872 edition of Wesley's *Works* translated the Latin to read: "I did not desert her: I did not send her away: I will not recall her."[22]

Much more could be said, and has been said in other books, about Wesley's miserable marriage. The point here is simply that he did not marry without first seeking the counsel of trusted advisors. Unfortunately, Charles, the one counselor who might have prevented this unhappy marriage, played such a key role in his brother's earlier experience of a broken heart that he was not consulted the second time.

The most significant relationship in a leader's life is with his or her spouse. A marriage partner who is fully engaged in or, at the very least, supportive of a spouse's work can be a significant contributor. Many promising leaders, eager to pour themselves into ministry, have been held back by a spouse who was reluctant about or even resistant to the work.

There are no guarantees when it comes to matters of the heart. Wesley's rule for team members could provide no guarantee of a happy marriage. What it could do was measure their willingness to be accountable in even the most personal concerns.

That may seem an unusually high level of accountability. Should you, if not yet married, really seek the counsel of other spiritual leaders before taking that step? Let's consider it another way: Why wouldn't you want the best possible advice on one of the biggest decisions of your life? Would you buy a house without consulting a realtor, a building inspector, and an appraiser? Would you buy a new car without checking *Consumer Reports*? King Solomon's book of Proverbs reminds us of the wisdom of seeking counsel: "Plans go wrong for lack of advice; many advisers bring success. . . . So don't go to war without wise guidance; victory depends on having many advisers" (Prov. 15:22; 24:6 NLT). Getting married does not, or at least should not, have much in common with going to war—except that both are momentous decisions with long-lasting consequences.

If you want others to be accountable to you, you must set that example. If you are not already in an accountability relationship with some other leader or a governing board, that may be the single most important step you can take to safeguard your ministry.

LEAD ACCOUNTABLY

Damian Williams, founder of Leadership League in Pittsburgh and a long-time friend, talks about the value of being in relationship with people who have permission to tell you hard things. He works with leaders of family-owned businesses and entrepreneurs who have built significant enterprises. Some of them have nearly lost their families and their fortunes through unwise decisions. Too often, he finds that those leaders had no one in their lives to whom they were accountable. None of their business associates or friends had been granted the authority to say no to them. No one was permitted to tell them difficult truths that they likely did not wish to hear.

I am glad to be part of a connectional ministry. It is one of the great strengths that Wesley imparted to his Methodist tribes. I value accountability, perhaps because I know my own weaknesses very well. I am glad to be in a stream of Christianity that provides over-sight and requires mutual submission. Accountability is a safeguard only insofar as we choose to submit to it.

I pastored a church in Baton Rouge, Louisiana, in the late 1980s when Jim Bakker, a prominent televangelist, was exposed for fraud and moral failure. The most aggressive of Bakker's critics was another minister who served in the same denomination, Jimmy Swaggart, himself a televangelist with his offices just a few miles from our home. Swaggart publicly castigated Bakker for not sub-mitting to the disciplinary oversight of their denomination.

Several months later, Swaggart's own moral failure was revealed. In spite of his repeated exhortations to Bakker, Swaggart, too, refused to submit to the denomination's disciplinary process. Instead, he withdrew from the denomination and set up a procedure for restoration he controlled and that quickly returned him to pas-toral leadership. The result was confusion in the congregation and disappointment in the wider Christian community.

No one likes a double standard or changing the rules midgame. If you sign up for the team, wear the jersey. If you're on the team, play team ball. The writer to the Hebrews put it this way: "Obey your leaders and submit to them, for they are keeping watch over your souls, as those who will have to give an account. Let them do this with joy and not with groaning, for that would be of no advantage to you" (Heb. 13:17 ESV).

There is a clear correlation between our willingness to be accountable to others and the spiritual authority we have to call others into accountability. As stated earlier, "Remember! A Methodist preacher is to mind every point, great and small, in the Methodist discipline! Therefore you will need all the sense you have, and to have all your wits about you! . . . Act in all things, not according to your own will, but as a son in the gospel."[23] A leader without accountability is an accident waiting to happen. If you want to lead like Wesley, lead with accountability.

REFLECTION

1. To whom am I accountable as a leader? Who has permission to ask me the hard questions?

2. To what degree do I submit to accountability? Would those who follow me agree with my assessment of my openness to accountability?

3. What would those responsible for supervising me say about my willingness to be held accountable?

4. What practices have I established in my organization to ensure stronger levels of accountability? Where are there gaps I must address?

10

LEAD
PURPOSEFULLY

Make God's mission your highest priority.

"You have nothing to do but to save souls. Therefore
spend and be spent in this work. And go always, not only to
those that want you, but to those that want you most."

Someone has observed that the two most important days in your life are the day you are born and the day you find out why. The early Methodists had discovered why they were born and passionately pursued their mission. A sense of purpose energizes a team. That's why staying laser-focused on your organization's mission is vital. Mission drift kills effectiveness.

This is especially true in the church. Mission is not a secondary consideration in the church; it's the main thing. The church did not create itself. God designed it for the purpose of carrying out his mission. David J. Bosch wrote, "It is not the church which 'undertakes' mission; it is the *missio Dei* which constitutes the church."[1]

Jesus lived a life of purpose as evidenced by these statements he made about himself: "For this purpose I was born and for this purpose I have come into the world—to bear witness to the truth"

(John 18:37 ESV); "For even the Son of Man did not come to be served, but to serve, and to give his life as a ransom for many" (Mark 10:45); "For the Son of Man came to seek and to save the lost" (Luke 19:10). The apostle Paul summarized Christ's mission this way: "Here is a trustworthy saying that deserves full acceptance: Christ Jesus came into the world to save sinners—of whom I am the worst" (1 Tim. 1:15).

Countless books are published each year on living a life of purpose and leading organizations purposefully. Almost three centuries before the best-selling book *The Purpose Driven Life* appeared, John Wesley resolved to pursue the highest purpose with his life.

ADOPT GOD'S PURPOSE

When asked to explain what gave rise to Methodism, Wesley responded, "In 1729, two young men, reading their Bible, saw they could not be saved without holiness, followed after it, and incited others so to do. In 1737 they saw holiness comes by faith. They saw likewise, that men are justified before they are sanctified; but still holiness was their point."[2] To be saved was their initial concern, but they soon realized that holiness was essential to salvation. They realized that they could not be saved without holiness, that they were saved by faith for the purpose of becoming holy by faith, and that the inevitable fruit of a holy life would be the salvation of even more souls.

Like most university students, Wesley thought a lot about his future. He was committed to following Christ's commands as closely as possible. He and his band committed to follow Christ's example by serving others, especially the poor and prisoners. In this early journal entry, Wesley wrestles with the truth that works of charity are not an end in themselves:

Whether it does not concern all men of all conditions to imitate Him, as much as they can, "who went about doing good?"

Whether all Christians are not concerned in that command, "While we have time, let us do good to all men?"

Whether we shall not be more happy hereafter, the more good we do now?

Whether we can be happy at all hereafter, unless we have, according to our power, "fed the hungry, clothed the naked, visited those that are sick, and in prison"; and made all these actions subservient to a higher purpose, even the saving of souls from death?[3]

Good deeds are not intended to stand alone. They must serve a higher purpose. Saving souls from eternal, spiritual death is the transcendent mission, the ultimate objective. Wesley's own life-transforming experience gave him a clear sense that this was the purpose for which he had been born.

No rule carried more weight for Wesley's helpers than this one. Everything they did was to be aimed toward their primary purpose. Wesley pressed his team to be single-minded on the priority of saving souls. This was the one rule that grabbed my attention when I first read it as a young pastor. To be honest, my initial response was that I had plenty of other things to do. I had books to read, sermons to write, reports to file, phone calls to return, and committee meetings to chair. But these words of Wesley penetrated my heart and have stayed with me for more than thirty years. They remind me of the solemn obligation and sacred trust at the core of my life. I have been rescued to rescue others.

Every energy, every task, is to be focused on this one thing. Heaven is not impressed with our trophies. Eternity will not be fascinated with the size of our buildings or budgets. There is no Top

100 list of the fastest-growing churches on a scoreboard in heaven. We know those things, but sometimes we forget.

The only two things that will make it from this side of eternity to the next are the incorruptible Word of God and the immortal souls of people. These people, our relatives and friends, will spend eternity in one of only two possible destinations: heaven or hell. God's grace has provided all they need to arrive in heaven, but the only opportunity they will have to respond to that grace occurs on this side of the grave. "How, then, can they call on the one they have not believed in? And how can they believe in the one of whom they have not heard? And how can they hear without someone preaching to them" (Rom. 10:14)?

One skeptic asked Wesley about his intentions. He wanted to know where Wesley planned to lead these people in the Methodist movement.

"But I hear," added he, "you preach to a great number of people every night and morning. Pray, what would you do with them? Whither would you lead them? What religion do you preach? What is it good for?" I replied, "I do preach to as many as desire to hear, every night and morning. You ask, what I would do with them: I would make them virtuous and happy, easy in themselves, and useful to others. Whither would I lead them? To heaven; to God the Judge, the lover of all, and to Jesus the Mediator of the new covenant. What religion do I preach? The religion of love; the law of kindness brought to light by the gospel. What is this good for? To make all who receive it enjoy God and themselves: To make them like God; lovers of all; contented in their lives; and crying out at their death, in calm assurance, "O grave, where is thy victory! Thanks be unto God, who giveth me the victory, through my Lord Jesus Christ."[4]

DON'T BE DETERRED BY CRITICS

Wesley was sometimes questioned about his practice of preaching outdoors rather than in churches, but he saw it as essential to fulfilling his purpose. He had been shut out of the established church, but people still needed to hear the good news. "Field-preaching was therefore a sudden expedient, a thing submitted to, rather than chosen; and therefore submitted to, because I thought preaching even thus, better than not preaching at all: First, in regard to my own soul, because, 'a dispensation of the gospel being committed to me,' I did not dare 'not to preach the gospel:' Secondly, in regard to the souls of others, whom I everywhere saw 'seeking death in the error of their life'"[5]

Wesley would not be deterred from his purpose. His calling was clear: "I did not dare 'not to preach the gospel.'" The need was great and evident. He could not lightly dismiss the fate of the spiritually lost people he saw around him everywhere.

When criticized, Wesley questioned the motives of his opponents. Did they feel he had taken away a privilege that they desired for themselves? Were any of them standing in line to preach outdoors in every season of the year?

For who is there among you, brethren, that is willing (examine your own hearts) even to save souls from death at this price? Would not you let a thousand souls perish, rather than you would be the instruments of rescuing them thus? I do not speak now with regard to conscience, but to the inconveniences that must accompany it. Can you sustain them, if you would? Can you bear the summer sun to beat upon your naked head? Can you suffer the wintry rain or wind, from whatever quarter it blows? Are you able to stand in the open air without any covering or defence when God casteth abroad his snow like wool, or scattereth his hoar-frost like ashes? And yet these are some of the smallest inconveniences which accompany field-preaching. Far beyond all these, are the contradiction of sinners, the scoffs both of the great vulgar and the small; contempt and reproach of every kind; often more than verbal affronts, stupid, brutal violence, sometimes to the hazard of health, or limbs, or life. Brethren, do you envy us this honour? What, I pray, would buy you to be a field-preacher? Or what, think you, could induce any man of common sense to continue therein one year, unless he had a full conviction in himself that it was the will of God concerning him?[6]

Wesley fairly questioned the price these critics were willing to pay to reach lost people. If they would not endure the hardships of field preaching to reach those who never darkened the door of the church, they should stop hindering his efforts to do so: "We now do, for the good of poor souls, what you cannot, will not, dare not do: And we desire not that you should. But this one thing we may reasonably desire of you—Do not increase the difficulties, which are already so great, that, without the mighty power of God, we must sink under them. Do not assist in trampling down a little handful of men, who, for the present, stand in the gap between ten thousand poor wretches and destruction, till you find some others to take their places."[7]

When accused of violating church order by using lay people, not properly ordained by the Church of England, to carry out the preaching, teaching, and administrative work of the Methodist movement, Wesley again appealed to the priority of the mission. In response to the charge that "for these laymen to exhort at all is a violation of all order," Wesley wrote, "What is this order of which you speak? Will it serve instead of the knowledge and love of God? Will this order rescue those from the snare of the Devil, who are now taken captive at his will? Will it keep them who are escaped a little way, from turning back into Egypt? If not, how should I answer it to God, if, rather than violate I know not what order, I should sacrifice thousands of souls thereto? I dare not do it. It is at the peril of my own soul."[8]

The eternal souls of men and women were at stake. Wesley would not defer to a point of order when it might make the difference in someone's spiritual destiny. He and his team members were willing to stand in the gap and do what the ordained clergy of the day would not stoop to do:

> Let us be employed, not in the highest, but in the meanest, and not in the easiest, but the hottest, service. Ease and plenty we leave to those that want them. Let us go on in toil, in weariness, in painfulness, in cold or hunger, so we may but testify the gospel of the grace of God. The rich, the honourable, the great, we are thoroughly willing (if it be the will of our Lord) to leave to you. Only let us alone with the poor, the vulgar, the base, the outcasts of men. Take also to yourselves the saints of the world: But suffer us "to call sinners to repentance"; even the most vile, the most ignorant, the most abandoned, the most fierce and savage of whom we can hear. To these we will go forth in the name of our Lord, desiring nothing, receiving nothing of any man (save the bread we eat, while we are under his roof), and let it be seen whether. God hath sent us.[9]

Wesley's team enabled him to accomplish far more than he could have alone. He realized that the mission was too large for any one person to handle. If what you dream about is so small that you can accomplish it on your own, dream bigger. You may travel faster alone, but you can go farther with a team. Wesley knew, too, that leading a team is even more challenging than doing the work yourself: "Preaching twice or thrice a day is no burden to me at all; but the care of all the preachers and all the people is a burden indeed!"[10]

CHANGE TACTICS OFTEN, CHANGE PURPOSE NEVER

There is no advantage to having more people in the room if you are not working toward a common goal. A group is not a team. There is shared power in shared purpose. The key to maintaining alignment on your team is to be crystal clear about the mission: "Observe: It is not your business to preach so many times, and to take care of this or that society; but to save as many souls as you can; to bring as many sinners as you possibly can to repentance, and with all your power to build them up in that holiness without which they cannot see the Lord. And remember! A Methodist preacher is to mind every point, great and small, in the Methodist discipline! Therefore you will need all the sense you have, and to have all your wits about you!"[11] Wesley was not impressed with mere activity if those efforts failed to rescue the perishing and build them up in holiness. Whatever else the leaders of the movement might accomplish, if they failed in this objective, the cause was lost.

Wesley continually evaluated and worked to improve the methods used to reach and develop people. The conference served well for that purpose: "In 1744 I wrote to several clergymen, and to all who then served me as sons in the gospel, desiring them to meet me in London, and to give me their advice concerning the best method of carrying on the work of God."[12]

Wesley did not allow tradition to impede the mission. Of course, not everyone was pleased with change. Like leaders today, Wesley had his critics, and few things bring more criticism than initiating change. These words addressed to Wesley will sound familiar to leaders everywhere: "There were no such meetings when I came into the society first: And why should there now? I do not understand these things, and this changing one thing after another continually."[13]

No leader escapes the question "Why are you changing things?" And most will hear someone say, "If it's not broken, why fix it?" Wesley's wise answer to his critic is instructive for us: "It was easily answered: It is pity but they had been at first. But we knew not then either the need or the benefit of them. Why we use them, you will readily understand, if you read over the rules of the society. . . . We prevent, so far as in us lies, their growing formal or dead. We are always open to instruction; willing to be wiser every day than we were before, and to change whatever we can change for the better."[14]

Wesley acknowledged that the societies' methods had changed—and that he would have done it sooner if he had realized how beneficial the change would be. Wesley went on to urge that Methodists be as flexible in their tactics as they were steadfast in purpose. He argued for the Methodists to stay open to instruction and acknowledged that strategies were not dogma but were valuable only to the degree that they accomplished the movement's purpose. Wesley knew, too, that change was helpful to keep the movement fresh.

Anyone who has been around the church for more than a few years will know that something a church tries once is an experiment. Anything it does twice is an established practice. And whatever it does three times is a treasured tradition. And not every tradition is truly sacred. Even its staunchest defenders acknowledge that "the sacred hour" of eleven o'clock Sunday worship was established to allow previous generations of farmers time to milk their cows before heading to church.

Clarity of purpose and courage in its pursuit allow, even demand, that we be ruthless in evaluating tactics and in discarding any unproductive ones. Dr. Paul Borden, a friend and mentor of mine, has served as a consultant for more than five hundred churches. Many of those congregations are, in his assessment, "perfectly structured for ministry—if 1950 ever comes around again." Borden added, "Everyone knows that you can't keep doing the same thing and expect different results. The problem today is that you can't keep doing the same thing and expect the *same* results."

Culture changes. People change. Sadly, some leaders and churches resist change until it is too late. To lead like Wesley means being more committed to your purpose than to your program. The leader must make whatever changes necessary to reach people in the current context before the moment of opportunity is past. Clarity of purpose grounds those changes and keeps the movement on course. Dr. Scott Snook and Nick Craig, leadership scholars and consultants, made this observation in a *Harvard Business Review* article:

> Over the past five years, there's been an explosion of interest in purpose-driven leadership. Academics argue persuasively that an executive's most important role is to be a steward of the organization's purpose. Business experts make the case that purpose is a key to exceptional performance, while psychologists describe it as the pathway to greater well-being.
>
> Doctors have even found that people with purpose in their lives are less prone to disease. Purpose is increasingly being touted as the key to navigating the complex, volatile, ambiguous world we face today, where strategy is ever changing and few decisions are obviously right or wrong.[15]

Dr. Laurel Buckingham led Moncton Wesleyan Church in New Brunswick, Canada, for more than forty years. During that time, the congregation changed locations, approaches to ministry, and worship format and times. The church began new programs and shut down ineffective ones, and even changed musical styles, one of the most volatile changes a church can make. Many methods changed, but the purpose remained the same.

In 1976 Buckingham and the church board prayerfully crafted what became known as the "Manifesto." It reads in part:

> Since a manifesto is a "declaration of intention, purpose, and motive," may it be clearly understood that our goal, cause, and purpose is to be in harmony with God's goal, cause, and purpose, which is "to seek and to save those who were lost."
>
> We must use every possible method in every possible place at every possible time to reach every possible person for Christ. Everything we do and everything we are is to be used for that purpose.
>
> The problem that exists is best illustrated by the fact that many evangelical churches wholeheartedly agree with this emphasis, but their performance and preoccupation with secondary matters often betrays their lack of dedication to such a cause. If at any time leadership is made aware of any part of our church function that conflicts with that purpose, that part will be deleted.[16]

This manifesto served as the rallying cry for Moncton Wesleyan Church for nearly four decades, during which the church baptized more than a thousand new believers and grew in worship attendance from four hundred to nearly two thousand.

ESTABLISH YOUR PURPOSE EARLY

Mick and Mel Veach and their family are dear friends to us. They were pioneers in taking the gospel to Central Asia where they ministered in a predominantly Muslim country for a decade, establishing a network of underground house churches. From that base, it would be possible to develop teams of leaders to penetrate other countries in that region with the gospel.

The Veachs returned home in 2006, and for the next nine years, Mick pastored Stoney Creek Community Church in suburban Detroit, which became one of the fastest-growing churches in Michigan, mobilizing dozens of workers for short-term and long-term international missions.

Mick and I were sitting in a restaurant on a Monday morning in 2014 when he shared a new vision that God had placed on his heart. A few months later, Mick resigned his comfortable position as senior leader in a growing church to plunge into the urban core of Detroit and plant Mosaic Church, a congregation strategically positioned to reach that diverse community. An amazing multiethnic congregation now flourishes in Detroit because Mick was driven by a purpose larger than himself and more lasting than his retirement account. Thousands of people will make eternity their home because my friend never lost sight of the mission and lived purposefully.

That commitment to a higher purpose did not materialize in a restaurant conversation in 2014. Mick Veach's life purpose had been established years earlier. When Mick became a Christ-follower, his youth pastor convinced him of the importance of living on purpose. Mick resonated with the apostle Paul's declaration in Acts 20:24 and made it his life verse: "However, I consider my life worth nothing to me; my only aim is to finish the race and complete the task the Lord Jesus has given me—the task of testifying to the good news of God's grace."

After graduating from Taylor University, Mick accepted a solo mission appointment in Columbia, South America. There, as a twenty-one-year-old, Mick hammered out this purpose statement for his life: To live out the life of Jesus, reach an unreached people group, and mobilize and disciple laborers for the harvest!

That concise statement of purpose guided Mick on dozens of trips around the globe. He lived it out. Eventually, Mick's commitment to that purpose led him into the heart of one of the neediest cities in North America. To lead like Wesley is to lead purposefully.

LEAD PURPOSEFULLY

When Wesley encountered leaders who were reluctant to give up their time of study to engage in personal conversations with people who were seeking God, he challenged them to reconsider their priorities as follows:

1. Gaining knowledge is a good thing; but saving souls is a better.

2. By this very thing you will gain the most excellent knowledge, that of God and eternity.

3. You will have time for gaining other knowledge too, if you spend all your mornings therein. Only sleep not more than you need; and never be idle, or triflingly employed. . . .

4. If you can do but one, let your studies alone. I would throw by all the libraries in the world, rather than be guilty of the loss of one soul.[17]

To lead purposefully, you must know what is most important and choose to put it first. You may have twenty items on your to-do list, but which of those will make a difference in someone's eternal destiny? The agenda for your monthly team meeting may have a dozen discussion items, but some of them will not make much difference in achieving the Great Commission.

Wesley instructed his field director in each of the societies to read this reminder every year as they engaged in fund-raising for the

Methodist school in Kingswood: "The wisdom and love of God have now thrust out a large number of labourers into His harvest; men who desire nothing on earth but to promote the glory of God, by saving their own souls and those that hear them."[18] Wesley led purposefully and called his team to do the same. They desired nothing but saving souls, their own souls and those of their hearers, all to promote God's glory.

The purpose of leadership is not to secure our comfort or protect our preferences. Leadership is a sacred trust given not for our benefit but to advance the mission of God:

> You and I are called to this; to save souls from death; to watch over them as those that must give an account! If our office implied no more than preaching a few times in a week, I could play with it: So might you. But how small a part of our duty (yours as well as mine) is this! God says to you, as well as me, "Do all thou canst, be it more or less, to save the souls for whom my Son has died." Let this voice be ever sounding in our ears; then shall we give up our account with joy. . . . I am ashamed of my indolence and inactivity. The good Lord help us both! Your business, as well as mine, is to save souls. When we took priests' orders, we undertook to make it our one business. I think every day lost, which is not (mainly at least) employed in this thing."[19]

A team that knows what matters most is incredibly powerful. When you know what that one thing is and desire nothing else, something dynamic is unleashed in the world. It can change a church, a community, even a nation. Lead purposefully, like Wesley, and see what God will do through you.

REFLECTION

1. How would the people closest to me describe what I am trying to accomplish?

2. How clear are my team members about the purpose of our organization?

3. In what ways am I making God's mission my highest priority? What am I doing to consistently build relationships with the people God is seeking?

4. If I'm not presently building relationships to become a "friend of sinners," what steps will I take to realign my time and energy to do so? To whom will I make myself accountable for this commitment?

CONCLUSION
MAKING A DIFFERENCE TODAY

Whether you have read this book alone in one sitting or over several meetings with your small group or leadership team, at some point you are going to ask, "So, now what do I do?" Information, by itself, is not worth much. Application of information can be life changing.

Hopefully, you now know a bit more about John Wesley and the early days of the Methodist movement in England. Their story is phenomenal and illustrates how God can use a few committed people to dramatically change the course of a nation. The work of those Methodist leaders continues to influence over seventy-five million people after more than three centuries.

APPLY WESLEY'S RULES

This book is intended to be more than a history lesson. To lead like Wesley, you must diligently apply his leadership theories to your life and ministry context. The principles Wesley hammered out in the fires of ministry hold their edge today. Technology has changed dramatically since Wesley's day; human nature remains amazingly the same. People are still the greatest resource, and sometimes the biggest headache, in any organization.

Leadership is about people. You don't lead buildings. You don't cast vision to spreadsheets. You don't have to encourage computers. But the people in the buildings, the accountants behind the spreadsheets and the programmers in front of the computers, all respond to great leadership. That is true in the marketplace and it is true in the church. People do not blindly follow your directions simply because you have a title. Now, more than ever, you must earn the right to lead.

Leading diligently mattered in Wesley's day, and it still makes a difference today. The most brilliant plans are worthless without implementation. Do what matters.

Leading urgently remains one of the best ways to capture attention. When the leader models a lack of urgency, you are certain to find complacency among those on the front line. Make every day count.

Lead positively because attitudes are contagious. If you are the leader, your thermostat sets your organization's temperature. Believe the best about everyone.

Lead candidly. Gossip is a culture-killer. Don't allow it to spread. To build trust with those in the room, be loyal to those who are not there. Or, as Wesley said, "Of the dead and the absent, [speak] nothing but good!"[1]

Leadership and responsibility cannot be separated. As leaders, we are caretakers of the culture. We must be willing to confront destructive behavior. Confront lovingly, clearly, and promptly. Feedback is the real breakfast of champions.

If you are the leader, lead humbly. God gives grace to the humble but leaves the proud to look out for themselves. Be less concerned about impressing people than with serving them.

If you are going to lead, lead boldly. Keep your heart clear, your hands clean, your eyes focused, and your passion hot. Leadership is not for the faint of heart. Give it your best. Join the apostle Paul in his determination and focus: "To this end I strenuously contend with all the energy Christ so powerfully works in me" (Col. 1:29).

Lead consistently. That doesn't make you boring. Rather, it establishes clear expectations that generate more freedom for your team to work creatively. Predictability builds confidence, and confidence invites creativity, so lead consistently.

Accountability is essential. If you're going to play on a team, play by the rules. Team members have a right to expect that from one another. The best leaders welcome accountability and require it of others.

The mission is the main thing. To lead like Wesley is to lead purposefully. The apostle Paul stressed the importance of keeping your eye on the prize: "Therefore I do not run like someone running aimlessly; I do not fight like a boxer beating the air" (1 Cor. 9:26).

I have coached and consulted with leaders in more than one hundred congregations in Australia, Canada, New Zealand, and the United States. Far too many churches in the Western world are stagnant or in decline. Maybe your church is one of them. There are many symptoms of church decline, but the most common cause is mission drift. Churches lose sight of their purpose.

Theologian Emil Brunner wrote these frequently quoted words: "The church exists by mission, just as a fire exists by burning."[2] He wrote those words in 1931, and they are still as true today as they were then. Any organization, including a church, that loses clarity about its mission is in danger of losing its fire. Once the fire is lost, the organization is on borrowed time. No rule Wesley offered is more important than the injunction to be purposeful. To put it another way: "The main thing is to keep the main thing the main thing."

GUARD AGAINST MISSION DRIFT

Guarding against mission drift may be your greatest challenge as a leader. It is a problem Wesley himself foresaw in the days before his death. The effective leadership Wesley developed through his organizational structure and these "Rules of a Helper" accelerated the Methodist movement to a degree of success and influence that even its critics reluctantly acknowledged. In 1786, at the age of eighty-three, Wesley looked back upon the movement he had shaped and then looked forward to the generations to come. He penned these words in his "Thoughts upon Methodism":

I am not afraid that the people called Methodists should ever cease to exist. . . . But I am afraid lest they should only exist as a dead sect, having the form of religion without the power. And this undoubtedly will be the case, unless they hold fast both the doctrine, spirit, and discipline with which they first set out. . . .

I fear, wherever riches have increased (exceeding few are the exceptions), the essence of religion, the mind that was in Christ, has decreased in the same proportion. Therefore, do I not see how it is possible, in the nature of things, for any revival of true religion to continue long. For religion must necessarily produce both industry and frugality; and these cannot but produce riches. But as riches increase, so will pride, anger, and love of the world in all its branches.

How, then, is it possible that Methodism, that is the religion of the heart, though it flourishes now as a green bay-tree, should continue in this state? For the Methodists in every place grow diligent and frugal; consequently, they increase in goods. Hence they proportionably [*sic*] increase in pride, in anger, in the desire of the flesh, the desire of the eyes, and the pride of life. So, although the form of religion remains, the spirit is swiftly vanishing away.

Is there no way to prevent this? This continual declension of pure religion? We ought not to forbid people to be diligent and frugal: We must exhort all Christians to gain all they can, and to save all they can; that is, in effect, to grow rich! What way, then (I ask again), can we take, that our money may not sink us to the nethermost hell? There is one way, and there is no other under heaven. If those who "gain all they can," and "save all they can," will likewise "give all they can"; then, the more they gain, the more they will grow in grace, and the more treasure they will lay up in heaven.[3]

Wesley feared that the success of the Methodist movement might ultimately lead to its downfall. God blessed the Methodists precisely because they were focused on reaching every person with the gospel and on striving earnestly to transform society. That blessing had the added benefit of creating material prosperity, to which many of the early Methodists were unaccustomed. Wesley feared that, preoccupied with their own comfort, they might lose sight of their purpose. He realized that the leader's task is to guard constantly against mission drift.

The apostle Paul stayed focused on his mission. He wrote to the Philippians about the trajectory of his life in Christ: "Not that I have already obtained all this, or have already arrived at my goal, but I press on to take hold of that for which Christ Jesus took hold of me. Brothers and sisters, I do not consider myself yet to have taken hold of it. But one thing I do: Forgetting what is behind and straining toward what is ahead, I press on toward the goal to win the prize for which God has called me heavenward in Christ Jesus" (Phil. 3:12–14). Leaders must model intentionality in their own lives and then embed that clarity of mission in the very fiber of their organization.

BE FILLED WITH LOVE

Beyond the leadership principles and even the power of staying focused on the mission, there is a critical aspect of leadership that many overlook. Without it, no amount of skill or effort will suffice. To lead like Wesley, you must be filled with the love of God.

Learning to lead like Wesley will stretch you to your limits. In fact, it may be part of God's plan to bring you to the end of your own abilities. Wesley had innate leadership abilities even before his heart-warming experience on Aldersgate Street on May 24, 1738. His temperament, intelligence, energy, and discipline attracted the attention of his colleagues at Oxford. The business investors who backed the Georgia colony selected Wesley as a missionary because his gifts and talents were obvious. However, Wesley himself did not always live up to his own ideals or potential.

You need something more than natural ability to lead like Wesley aspired to lead. John Wesley received clear assurance of salvation by faith that May evening on Aldersgate Street as he listened to a Bible study leader read from Luther's commentary on the book of Romans. After that he experienced a divine strength that went beyond temperament or training. And Wesley had ongoing encounters with the Holy Spirit that became a unique thread in the message of the Methodist movement.

Wesley believed that Jesus Christ came to offer more than a good example and sound teaching. Wesley became convinced that the sinless life, sacrificial death, and triumphant resurrection of Christ had transformative power for every person who believed— that God, through his Holy Spirit, could change a human being's heart. What was that fundamental change that Wesley experienced and coveted for others? It was love.

Love was the secret to Wesley's leadership. The God of love brought new life to Wesley, a life characterized by love for God and others. In response to God, that love motivated faith and obedience. Toward others, love became cheerful service. As the apostle Paul put it, "Hope does not put us to shame, because God's love has been poured out into our hearts through the Holy Spirit, who has been given to us" (Rom. 5:5). Love is not something you work up. It is something God pours in.

Wesley's essay "A Farther Appeal to Men of Reason and Religion" offers this insight: "What tender love to the whole of human kind, will you drink in, together with the love of God, from the unexhausted source of love! And how easy is it to conceive that more and more of his image will be then transfused into your soul; that from disinterested love, all other divine tempers will, as it were naturally, spring: Mildness, gentleness, patience, temperance, justice, sincerity, contempt of the world; yea, whatsoever things are venerable and lovely, whatsoever are justly of good report!"[4]

Love is the secret. To love God with your whole heart and your neighbor as yourself is the essence of leading like Wesley. This is the heart of leadership. It means choosing to see others as deeply loved by God and therefore worthy of your love. And if you love others, you are willing to serve them at all costs.

The danger in following Wesley's rules for leadership is that you could think of them as just a checklist, one more list of habits to be practiced mindlessly or even reluctantly. It would be a mistake to see Wesley's methodical approach as dispassionate or heartless. To lead like Wesley is to be motivated by love. This is the impulse for leadership in God's kingdom. If you are running low on love, digging deeper and trying harder will be of no value. This love is not a sentimental emotion that can be conjured up with warm thoughts and soft music. God's love is something much deeper, and he alone is the source.

Dr. Jo Anne Lyon, founder of World Hope International and the first woman to serve as general superintendent of The Wesleyan Church, is an amazing leader. She is known for bold vision and tireless energy. But what most people notice about her immediately is her obvious love for others. She has been invited to consult with political leaders at the very highest levels of power, yet she just as willingly listens attentively to a young child or elderly grandmother. She remembers people's names and the stories of their lives because she genuinely cares about them.

I participated in a meeting with Dr. Lyon and a group of leaders when she confessed that this had not always been the case. She shared that in the early days of their marriage, she and her husband, Wayne, served a church that included a group of people she was finding it difficult to love—or even like. The tension of living and serving in that situation became so draining that she was tempted to give up on both their ministry and their marriage. Finally, she reached a breaking point. She realized she could not change her feelings toward those people. She needed God to change her heart. She cried out to God in hours of desperate prayer, confessing her brokenness and seeking God's mercy. God heard her prayer. She experienced a fresh filling of the Holy Spirit. What was the first evidence? Love.

Dr. Lyon went on to tell of the change in her attitude toward the people she had found so difficult. During a midweek prayer service, just a few days after this powerful experience with God, she noticed a dramatic difference in how she related to those same people. They had not changed, but something had changed in her. God had poured his love into her heart, and that love flowed out to the people around her.

You do not have to love people to lead them in many contexts. You may be able to exert positional authority to ensure cooperation. It may be possible for you to influence their behavior through financial rewards or even intimidation. But how long does that sort of leadership last? When you no longer hold that power, people will no longer follow.

To lead as Wesley led, you must have something more than a title, a budget, and the latest management theory. You must have a heart filled with love. You will never realize your full potential as a leader, or that of your organization, until you love the people you serve. You will lead stronger and your influence will last longer if you are able to put their interests ahead of your own.

Wesley often noted his affection for the Methodist people. Here is one example from his journal, a note made while ministering in Nottingham: "I preached to a numerous and well-behaved congregation. I love this people: There is something wonderfully pleasing, both in their spirit and their behaviour."[5] Journaling from the Isle of Wight on October 9, 1782, Wesley noted his belief that the door was open to press the cause further. The only thing lacking was leaders with faith and love: "This place seems now ripe for the gospel: Opposition is at an end. Only let our preachers be men of faith and love, and they will see the fruit of their labours."[6]

More love was Wesley's constant prayer. After a conference of Methodist leaders in London on August 16, 1767, he reported God's blessing on this meeting with stewards, assistants, and local preachers: "Love and harmony reigned from the beginning to the end; but we have all need of more love and holiness; and, in order thereto, of crying continually, 'Lord, increase our faith!'"[7]

My goal is that you take away from this book more than a few helpful insights on leadership. I hope God has used these pages to cultivate within you a hunger to more effectively serve God and others with your abilities. And I pray you will understand that you cannot do this in your own strength. May God keep on filling you with his Holy Spirit until you overflow with his divine love. Only then can you lead like Wesley.

APPENDIX A

WESLEY'S TWELVE RULES OF A HELPER

What follows is John Wesley's response to the question, "What are the rules of a helper?" as recorded in his "Minutes of Several Conversations":

1. Be diligent. Never be unemployed a moment. Never be triflingly employed. Never while away time; neither spend more time at any place than is strictly necessary.

2. Be serious. Let your motto be, "Holiness to the Lord." Avoid all lightness, jesting, and foolish talking.

3. Converse sparingly and cautiously with women; particularly, with young women.

4. Take no step toward marriage, without first consulting with your brethren.

5. Believe evil of no one; unless you see it done, take heed how you credit it. Put the best construction on everything. You know the Judge is always supposed to be on the prisoner's side.

6. Speak evil of no one; else your word especially would eat as doth a canker. Keep your thoughts within your own breast, till you come to the person concerned.

7. Tell every one what you think wrong in him, and that plainly, as soon as may be; else it will fester in your heart. Make all haste to cast the fire out of your bosom.

8. Do not affect the gentleman. . . . A preacher of the gospel is the servant of all.

9. Be ashamed of nothing but sin: Not of fetching wood (if time permit) or drawing water; not of cleaning your own shoes, or your neighbour's.

10. Be punctual. Do everything exactly at the time. And in general, do not mend our Rules, but keep them; not for wrath, but for conscience' sake.

11. You have nothing to do but to save souls. Therefore spend and be spent in this work. And go always, not only to those that want you, but to those that want you most. . . .

12. Act in all things, not according to your own will, but as a son in the gospel. As such, it is your part to employ your time in the manner which we direct; partly, in preaching and visiting from house to house; partly, in reading, meditation, and prayer. Above all, if you labour with us in our Lord's vineyard, it is needful that you should do that part of the work which we advise, at those times and places which we judge most for his glory.[1]

APPENDIX B

WHO ARE METHODISTS?

What follows is an excerpt from John Wesley's "Advice to the People Called Methodists":

By Methodists I mean, a people who profess to pursue (in whatsoever measure they have attained) holiness of heart and life, inward and outward conformity in all things to the revealed will of God; who place religion in an uniform resemblance of the great object of it; in a steady imitation of Him they worship, in all his imitable perfections; more particularly, in justice, mercy, and truth, or universal love filling the heart, and governing the life.

You, to whom I now speak, believe this love of human kind cannot spring but from the love of God. You think there can be no instance of one whose tender affection embraces every child of man (though not endeared to him either by ties of blood, or by any natural or civil relation), unless that affection flow from a grateful, filial love to the common Father of all; to God, considered not only as his Father, but as "the Father of the spirits of all flesh"; yea, as the general Parent and Friend of all the families both of heaven and earth.

This filial love you suppose to flow only from faith, which you describe as a supernatural evidence (or conviction) of things not seen; so that to him who has this principle,

> The things unknown to feeble sense,
> Unseen by reason's glimmering ray,
> With strong commanding evidence
> Their heavenly origin display.
>
> Faith lends its realizing light,
> The clouds disperse, the shadows fly;
> The' Invisible appears in sight,
> And God is seen by mortal eye.

You suppose this faith to imply an evidence that God is merciful to me a sinner; that he is reconciled to me by the death of his Son, and now accepts me for his sake. You accordingly describe the faith of a real Christian as "a sure trust and confidence" (over and above his assent to the sacred writings) "which he hath in God, that his sins are forgiven; and that he is, through the merits of Christ, reconciled to the favour of God."

You believe, farther, that both this faith and love are wrought in us by the Spirit of God; nay, that there cannot be in any man one good temper or desire, or so much as one good thought, unless it be produced by the almighty power of God, by the inspiration or influence of the Holy Ghost.

If you walk by this rule, continually endeavouring to know and love and resemble and obey the great God and Father of our Lord Jesus Christ, as the God of love, of pardoning mercy; if from this principle of loving, obedient faith, you carefully abstain from all evil, and labour, as you have opportunity, to do good to all men, friends or enemies; if, lastly, you unite together, to encourage and help each other in thus working out your salvation, and for that end watch over one another in love, you are they whom I mean by Methodists.[1]

NOTES

INTRODUCTION

1. "Fast Facts about American Religion," Hartford Institute for Religion Research, accessed January 6, 2016, http://hirr.hartsem.edu/research/fast facts/fast_facts.html#numcong.

2. "BBC TWO Reveals the Ten Greatest Britons of All Time," BBC, October 19, 2002, http://www.bbc.co.uk/pressoffice/pressreleases/stories/2002/10_october/19/great_britons.shtml.

3. "John Wesley: Did You Know?," Christian History, last updated January 1, 1983, http://www.christianitytoday.com/ch/1983/ issue2/204.html.

4. John Shorb, "John Wesley's The Primitive Physick: Q & A with Randy Maddox," Church Health, March 12, 2011, http://chreader.org/john-wesleys-primitive-physick/.

5. John H. Lenton, "John Wesley's Preachers," The United Methodist Church Archives & History, accessed January 6, 2016, http://www.gcah.org/history/john-wesleys-preachers.

6. Augustus Toplady, *The Works of Augustus Toplady: A New Edition, Complete in One Volume* (London: J. Chidley, 1837), 256, 279.

7. John Wesley, "Minutes of Several Conversations," in *The Works of John Wesley*, vol. 8, 3rd ed. (Kansas City, MO: Beacon Hill, 1979), 299.

8. Ibid., 313.

9. Ibid., 314–315.

10. Ibid., 315.

11. Ibid., 315–316.

12. Nicole Fallon Taylor, "35 Inspiring Leadership Quotes," Business News Daily, September 9, 2015, http://www.businessnews daily.com/7481-leadership-quotes.html#sthash.o47zWKEz.dpuf.

13. Wesley, *Works*, 309.

14. Ibid.

15. "Appendix 3: Rules of a Helper," The Methodist Church of Southern Africa, accessed January 6, 2016, http://www.methodist.org.za/publications/laws/appendix3.

16. A complimentary copy of *The Wesleyan Discipline*, 2012 edition, is available for online download at https://www.wesleyan.org/1590/complimentary-copy-of-the-discipline-available.

CHAPTER 1

1. John Wesley, "A Collection of Forms of Prayer," *The Works of John Wesley*, vol. 11, 3rd ed. (Kansas City, MO: Beacon Hill, 1979), 209.

2. "Barnes' New Testament Notes," Christian Classics Ethereal Library, accessed January 6, 2016, http://www.ccel.org/ccel/barnes/ntnotes.ix.xii.viii.html.

3. John Wesley, "Minutes of Several Conversations," *The Works of John Wesley*, vol. 8, 3rd ed. (Kansas City, MO: Beacon Hill, 1979), 323.

4. John Wesley, "On Redeeming the Time," *The Works of John Wesley*, vol. 7, 3rd ed. (Kansas City, MO: Beacon Hill, 1979), 68–69.

5. Peter Drucker, *The Effective Executive: The Definitive Guide to Getting the Right Things Done* (New York: HarperCollins, 2002).

6. Samuel Dunn, *The Life of Adam Clarke* (London: William Tegg, 1863), 104.

7. Charles Wesley, "Give Me the Faith Which Can Remove," 1749, public domain.

8. John Wooden and Jay Carty, *Coach Wooden One-on-One: Inspiring Conversations on Purpose, Passion and the Pursuit of Success* (Ventura, CA: Regal, 2003), 33.

9. John Wesley, "Journal," *The Works of John Wesley*, vol. 2, 3rd ed. (Kansas City, MO: Beacon Hill, 1979), 534.

10. Albert Schweitzer, "Quotes by Albert Schweitzer," The Albert Schweitzer Fellowship, accessed January 6, 2016, http://www.schweitzerfellowship.org/about/albert-schweitzer/quotes- by-albert-schweitzer/.

11. Thomas J. Watson, Sr., *American Druggist* 100 (1939): 40.

12. Ronald Heifetz, *Leadership without Easy Answers* (Cambridge, MA: Harvard University Press, 1994), 113.

CHAPTER 2

1. Louise Story, "Anywhere the Eye Can See, It's Likely to See an Ad," *The New York Times*, January 15, 2007, http://www.nytimes.com/2007/01/15/business/media/15everywhere.html?pagewanted=all&_r=1&.

2. John Wesley, "Letters to Mr. James Bogie," *The Works of John Wesley*, vol. 12, 3rd ed. (Kansas City, MO: Beacon Hill, 1979), 521.

3. Tom Peters, "Bias for Action" *TomPeters!* (blog), February 2012, http://tompeters.com/2012/02/bias-for-action/.

4. John Wesley, "Letters to Mr. John Smith," *The Works of John Wesley*, vol. 12, 3rd ed. (Kansas City, MO: Beacon Hill, 1979), 72.

5. John Wesley, "Letters to Mr. Hopper," *The Works of John Wesley*, vol. 12, 3rd ed. (Kansas City, MO: Beacon Hill, 1979), 306–307.

6. John P. Kotter, *A Sense of Urgency* (Boston: Harvard Business Press, 2008), 49.

7. Ibid., 115.

8. Jim Collins, *Good to Great: Why Some Companies Make the Leap . . . and Others Don't* (New York: HarperCollins, 2001), 142.

9. Wesley, "Letters to Mr. Hopper," *Works*, 305.

10. Cindy Wahler, "Can Leadership Urgency Be Taught?," *Forbes*, June 20, 2014, http://www.forbes.com/sites/85broads/2014/06/20/can-leadership-urgency-be-taught/.

11. John Wesley, "Letters to a Member of the Society," *The Works of John Wesley*, vol. 12, 3rd ed. (Kansas City, MO: Beacon Hill, 1979), 276.

12. Ibid., 282.

13. John Wesley, "Letters to a Young Disciple," *The Works of John Wesley*, vol. 12, 3rd ed. (Kansas City, MO: Beacon Hill, 1979), 440–441.

14. Winston Churchill, Goodreads, accessed January 20, 2016, http://www.goodreads.com/quotes/1999-for-myself-i-am-an-optimist---it-does-not.

15. Daniel Goleman, Richard Boyatzis, and Annie McKee, *Primal Leadership: Unleashing the Power of Emotional Intelligence*, 10th ann. ed. (Boston: Harvard Business School Publishing, 2013), 34–35.

16. John Wesley, "Journal," *The Works of John Wesley*, vol. 2, 3rd ed. (Kansas City, MO: Beacon Hill, 1979), 192.

17. Ibid., 43.

18. Wesley, "Letters to Mr. John Smith," *Works*, 83.

19. J. Oswald Sanders, *Spiritual Leadership: Principles of Excellence for Every Believer*, 2nd rev. (Chicago: Moody, 1994), 94.

20. Richard Baxter, *The Poetical Fragments of Richard Baxter*, 4th ed. (London: William Pickering, 1821), 35.

21. John Wesley, "Journal," *The Works of John Wesley*, vol. 4, 3rd ed. (Kansas City, MO: Beacon Hill, 1979), 14.

22. Ibid., 11.

23. Louise Robinson Chapmen, "Christian Commitment: My Colors," *Missions Mobilizer*, last updated February 10, 2015, http://home.snu.edu/~hculbert/commit.htm.

24. John Wesley, "Letters to Miss Bolton," *The Works of John Wesley*, vol. 12, 3rd ed. (Kansas City, MO: Beacon Hill, 1979), 483.

25. John Wesley, "Letters to Mr. John Valton," *The Works of John Wesley*, vol. 12, 3rd ed. (Kansas City, MO: Beacon Hill, 1979), 489.

26. Stephen Covey, *First Things First* (New York: Fireside, 1994), 37.

27. Sanders, *Spiritual Leadership*, 96.

28. Richard Baxter, "Miscellaneous Extracts," quoted in Epes Sargent, *The Standard Fourth Reader for Public and Private Schools* (Boston: Phillips, Sampson and Company, 1857), 275.

29. Wesley, "Letters to a Member of the Society," *Works*, 304.

CHAPTER 3

1. John Wesley, "Minutes of Several Conversations," *The Works of John Wesley*, vol. 8, 3rd ed. (Kansas City, MO: Beacon Hill, 1979), 309–310.

2. Charles Swindoll, *Strengthening Your Grip: How to Be Grounded in a Chaotic World*, rev. ed. (Brentwood, TN: Worthy, 2015), 227.

3. John Wesley, "Journal," *The Works of John Wesley*, vol. 4, 3rd ed. (Kansas City, MO: Beacon Hill, 1979), 4.

4. John Wesley, "Letters to Mr. Blackwell," *The Works of John Wesley*, vol. 12, 3rd ed. (Kansas City, MO: Beacon Hill, 1979), 169.

5. Ibid., 182.

6. Wesley, "Journal," *Works*, vol. 4, 47.

7. Wesley, "Letters to Mr. Blackwell," *Works*, 183.

8. John Wesley, "Journal," *The Works of John Wesley*, 3rd ed. (Kansas City, MO: Beacon Hill, 1979), 197.

9. Dan Reiland, *Amplified Leadership: 5 Practices to Establish Influence, Build People, and Impact Others* (Lake Mary, FL: Charisma House, 2011), 54–55.

10. John Maxwell, *Developing the Leader within You* (Nashville: Thomas Nelson, 1993), 67.

11. John Wesley, "Letters to Mr. Hopper," *The Works of John Wesley*, vol. 12, 3rd ed. (Kansas City, MO: Beacon Hill, 1979), 306.

12. Ibid.

13. John Wesley, "Letters to Mr. Thomas Rankin," *The Works of John Wesley*, vol. 12, 3rd ed. (Kansas City, MO: Beacon Hill, 1979), 325.

14. Wesley, "Journal," *Works*, vol. 2, 421.

15. Mark Miller, *The Heart of Leadership: Becoming a Leader People Want to Follow* (San Francisco: Berrett-Koehler, 2013), 45.

16. John Wesley, "Letters to Mr. John Smith," *The Works of John Wesley*, vol. 12, 3rd ed. (Kansas City, MO: Beacon Hill, 1979), 56–57.

17. John Wesley, "Letters to His Brother Charles," *The Works of John Wesley*, vol. 12, 3rd ed. (Kansas City, MO: Beacon Hill, 1979), 115.

18. Ibid., 122.

19. John Wesley, "Letter to ——," *The Works of John Wesley*, vol. 12, 3rd ed. (Kansas City, MO: Beacon Hill, 1979), 249.

20. Stephen Covey, *Principle-Centered Leadership* (New York: Free Press, 1991), 122–123.

21. Ibid., 59.

22. James Kouzes and Barry Posner, *The Leadership Challenge: How to Make Extraordinary Things Happen in Organizations*, 5th ed. (San Francisco: Jossey-Bass, 2012), 279.

23. John Wesley, "Letters to Mrs. Sarah Ryan," *The Works of John Wesley*, vol. 12, 3rd ed. (Kansas City, MO: Beacon Hill, 1979), 217.

CHAPTER 4

1. John Wesley, "Journal," *The Works of John Wesley*, vol. 1, 3rd ed. (Kansas City, MO: Beacon Hill, 1979), 301.

2. Ibid.

3. Ibid., 303.

4. John Wesley, "The Cure of Evil-Speaking," *The Works of John Wesley*, vol. 6, 3rd ed. (Kansas City, MO: Beacon Hill, 1979), 114–115.

5. John Wesley, "Minutes of Several Conversations," *The Works of John Wesley*, vol. 8, 3rd ed. (Kansas City, MO: Beacon Hill, 1979), 308.

6. John Wesley, "Letters to a Young Disciple," *The Works of John Wesley*, vol. 12, 3rd ed. (Kansas City, MO: Beacon Hill, 1979), 446.

7. John Wesley, "Journal," *The Works of John Wesley*, vol. 2, 3rd ed. (Kansas City, MO: Beacon Hill, 1979), 74.

8. John Wesley, "Letters to Miss Bishop," *The Works of John Wesley*, vol. 13, 3rd ed. (Kansas City, MO: Beacon Hill, 1979), 19.

9. John Wesley, "Repentance of Believers," *The Works of John Wesley*, vol. 5, 3rd ed. (Kansas City, MO: Beacon Hill, 1979), 161.

10. Stephen Covey, *The Speed of Trust: The One Thing That Changes Everything* (New York: Free Press, 2006), 6, 18.

11. Ibid., 21.

12. Wesley, "The Cure of Evil-Speaking," *Works*, 123.

13. Wesley, "Journal," *Works*, vol. 1, 302.

14. John Wesley, "Journal," *The Works of John Wesley*, vol. 4, 3rd ed. (Kansas City, MO: Beacon Hill, 1979), 203.

15. Ibid., 29.

16. Covey, *The Speed of Trust*, 168.

17. Joel B. Green, *Reading Scripture as Wesleyans* (Nashville: Abingdon, 2010), 10.

18. Wesley, "Minutes of Several Conversations," *Works*, 323.

19. John Wesley, "Letters to ——," *The Works of John Wesley*, vol. 12, 3rd ed. (Kansas City, MO: Beacon Hill, 1979), 250–251.

20. Wesley, "Journal," *Works*, vol. 1, 86.

21. John Wesley, "Rules of the Band-Societies," *The Works of John Wesley*, vol. 8, 3rd ed. (Kansas City, MO: Beacon Hill, 1979), 272.

22. Ibid., 272–273.

23. John Wesley, "The More Excellent Way," *The Works of John Wesley*, vol. 7, 3rd ed. (Kansas City, MO: Beacon Hill, 1979), 33.

24. "Yik Yak App: Why Schools Are Concerned," CBC News, last updated January 21, 2015, http://www.cbc.ca/news/technology/yik-yak-app-why-schools-are-concerned-1.2920155.

CHAPTER 5

1. Winston Churchill, "The Gift of a Common Tongue" (lecture, Harvard University, Cambridge, MA, September 6, 1943), accessed December 21, 2015, http://www.winstonchurchill.org/resources/speeches/1941-1945-war-leader/420-the-price-of-greatness-is-responsibility.

2. John Wesley, "Journal," *The Works of John Wesley*, vol. 2, 3rd ed. (Kansas City, MO: Beacon Hill, 1979), 507–508.

3. John Wesley, "Letters to Mr. John Trembath," *The Works of John Wesley*, vol. 12, 3rd ed. (Kansas City, MO: Beacon Hill, 1979), 215–253.

4. Ibid., 253.

5. Ibid., 254.

6. John Wesley, "Letters to a Member of the Society," *The Works of John Wesley*, vol. 12, 3rd ed. (Kansas City, MO: Beacon Hill, 1979), 289.

7. Wesley, "Journal," *Works*, 142.

8. John Wesley, "The Letters of John Wesley," Wesley Center Online, accessed January 8, 2016, http://wesley.nnu.edu/john-wesley/the-letters-of-john-wesley/wesleys-letters-1762/.

9. Ken Blanchard and Spencer Johnson, *The One Minute Manager* (New York: William Morrow and Company, 1982).

10. Kerry Patterson et al, *Crucial Conversations: Tools for Talking When Stakes Are High*, 2nd ed. (New York: McGraw-Hill, 2012), 9–10.

11. Wesley, "Journal," *Works*, 132.

12. James Kouzes and Barry Posner, *Encouraging the Heart: A Leader's Guide to Rewarding and Recognizing Others* (San Francisco: Jossey-Bass, 2003), xi.

13. John Wesley, "Letters to Robert C. Brackenbury, Esq.," *The Works of John Wesley*, vol. 13, 3rd ed. (Kansas City, MO: Beacon Hill, 1979), 7.

14. Blanchard and Johnson, *One Minute Manager*, 94.

15. Wesley, "Journal," *Works*, 10.

16. Ibid., 512.

17. Ibid.

18. Ibid., 54.

19. Ibid., 54–55.

20. John Wesley, "Letters to Mr. Zechariah Yewdall," *The Works of John Wesley*, vol. 13, 3rd ed. (Kansas City, MO: Beacon Hill, 1979), 13.

21. John Trembath, "Letter 546," in *The Arminian Magazine for the Year 1790*, vol. 13 (London, 1790), 557.

22. Dietrich Bonhoeffer, *Letters and Papers from Prison*, ed. Eberhard Bethge, enl. ed. (New York: Touchstone, 1971), 298.

CHAPTER 6

1. Williams O'Flaherty, "Quotes Not by C. S. Lewis: A Preliminary Examination," Essential C. S. Lewis, last updated October 12, 2015, http://www.essential cslewis.com/2014/01/26/quotes-not-by-lewis-a-preliminary-examination/.

2. John Wesley, "Letters to Mr. John Trembath," *The Works of John Wesley*, vol. 12, 3rd ed. (Kansas City, MO: Beacon Hill, 1979), 251.

3. John Wesley, "Letters to a Member of the Society," *The Works of John Wesley*, vol. 12, 3rd ed. (Kansas City, MO: Beacon Hill, 1979), 301.

4. John Wesley, "Letter to a Friend," *The Works of John Wesley*, vol. 12, 3rd ed. (Kansas City, MO: Beacon Hill, 1979), 38–39.

5. John Wesley, "Life of Mr. Fletcher," *The Works of John Wesley*, vol. 11, 3rd ed. (Kansas City, MO: Beacon Hill, 1979), 342.

6. Ibid., 342–343.

7. Ibid., 343.

8. Ibid., 363.

9. Abraham Lincoln, quoted in John C. Maxwell, *Ultimate Leadership: Maximize Your Potential and Empower Your Team* (Nashville: Thomas Nelson, 2007), 486.

10. Lazlo Bock, quoted in Jeanine Prime and Elizabeth Salib, "The Best Leaders Are Humble Leaders," *Harvard Business Review*, May 12, 2014, https://hbr.org/2014/05/the-best-leaders-are-humble-leaders.

11. Jim Collins, *Good to Great: Why Some Companies Make the Leap . . . and Others Don't* (New York: HarperCollins, 2001), 39.

12. Steve Gutzler, "The Single Greatest Quality of Leadership," *Steve Gutzler—Leadership Quest* (blog), accessed January 7, 2016, http://www.stevegutzler. com/blog-steve-gutzler/2015/2/3/the-single-greatest-quality-of-leadership.

13. Thomas à Kempis, *The Imitation of Christ*, trans. Leo Sherley-Price (London: Pengiun, 1952), 32.

14. John Wesley, "Forms of Prayer," *The Works of John Wesley*, vol. 11, 3rd ed. (Kansas City, MO: Beacon Hill, 1979), 214, 216–217.

15. Ibid., 216.

16. Richard Green, *John Wesley: Evangelist* (London: The Religious Tract Society, 1905), 335–336.

17. Andrew Murray, quoted in Roy B. Zuck, *The Speaker's Quote Book: Over 5,000 Illustrations and Quotations for All Occasions* (Grand Rapids, MI: Kregel, 2009), 269.

18. Martin Luther, *Martin Luther's Christmas Book*, ed. Roland H. Bainton (Minneapolis, MN: Augsburg, 1948), 20.

CHAPTER 7

1. John Wesley, "The Letters of John Wesley," Wesley Center Online, accessed January 8, 2016, http://wesley.nnu.edu/john-wesley/the-letters-of-john-wesley/wesleys-letters-1777/.

2. John Wesley, "Journal," *The Works of John Wesley*, vol. 2, 3rd ed. (Kansas City, MO: Beacon Hill, 1979), 113–114.

3. Ibid., 262.

4. Ibid., 258.

5. Ibid., 259.

6. John Wesley, "Journal," *The Works of John Wesley*, vol. 3, 3rd ed. (Kansas City, MO: Beacon Hill, 1979), 23.

7. Wesley, "Journal," *Works*, vol. 2, 19.

8. Ibid., 33.

9. Ibid., 187.

10. Ibid., 61.

11. Ibid., 207.

12. Ibid., 190.

13. Ibid., 111–112.

14. Ibid., 172.

15. Ibid., 10.

16. Ibid., 9.

17. John Wesley, "Journal," *The Works of John Wesley*, vol. 4, 3rd ed. (Kansas City, MO: Beacon Hill, 1979), 30.

18. Brené Brown, *Daring Greatly: How the Courage to Be Vulnerable Transforms the Way We Live, Love, Parent, and Lead* (New York: Gotham Books, 2012), 65–66.

19. J. Oswald Sanders, *Spiritual Leadership: Principles of Excellence for Every Believer*, 2nd rev. (Chicago: Moody, 1994), 127–128.

20. Larry Alex Taunton, "Listening to Young Atheists: Lessons for a Stronger Christianity," *The Atlantic*, June 6, 2013, http://www.theatlantic.com/national/archive/2013/06/listening-to-young-atheists-lessons-for-a-stronger-christianity/276584/.

21. Billy Graham, "Courage to Stand," Billy Graham Evangelistic Association, June 8, 2015, http://billygraham.org/devotion/ courage-to-stand/.

22. Elisabeth Elliot, *Shadow of the Almighty: The Life & Testament of Jim Elliot* (New York: HarperCollins, 1958), 79.

23. Roland H. Bainton, *Here I Stand: A Life of Martin Luther* (Nashville: Abingdon, 1978), 181–182.

24. Seth Godin, *Tribes: We Need You to Lead Us* (New York: Penguin, 2008), 55.

CHAPTER 8

1. John Wesley, "Minutes of Several Conversations," *The Works of John Wesley*, vol. 8, 3rd ed. (Kansas City, MO: Beacon Hill, 1979), 317.

2. John Wesley, "Journal," *The Works of John Wesley*, vol. 3, 3rd ed. (Kansas City, MO: Beacon Hill, 1979), 46.

3. Will Durant, *The Story of Philosophy: The Lives and Opinions of the World's Greatest Philosophers from Plato to John Dewey* (New York: Pocket Books, 1961), 98.

4. John Dryden, IZ Quotes, accessed January 8, 2016, http://izquotes.com/quote/53385.

5. Wesley, "Minutes of Several Conversations," *Works*, 322.

6. John Wesley, "Journal," *The Works of John Wesley*, vol. 2, 3rd ed. (Kansas City, MO: Beacon Hill, 1979), 88.

7. Ibid., 58.

8. Wesley, "Journal," *Works*, vol. 3, 7.

9. John Wesley, "Journal," *The Works of John Wesley*, vol. 4, 3rd ed. (Kansas City, MO: Beacon Hill, 1979), 21.

10. Wesley, "Minutes of Several Conversations," *Works*, 300.

11. Wesley, "Journal," *Works*, vol. 3, 184.

12. Ibid., 119.

13. John Wesley, "Letter to the Rev. Mr. D——," *The Works of John Wesley*, vol. 12, 3rd ed. (Kansas City, MO: Beacon Hill, 1979), 264.

14. John Wesley, "A Plain Account of the People Called Methodists," *The Works of John Wesley*, vol. 8, 3rd ed. (Kansas City, MO: Beacon Hill, 1979), 254.

15. Warren Wiersbe, "Principles Are the Bottom Line," *Leadership Journal*, Christianity Today Library, January 1, 1980, http://www.ctlibrary.com/le/1980/winter/80l1081.html.

16. John Wesley, "Letters to Mr. Walter Churchey," *The Works of John Wesley*, vol. 12, 3rd ed. (Kansas City, MO: Beacon Hill, 1979), 438.

17. Adam Bryant, "In Head-Hunting, Big Data May Not Be Such a Big Deal," *The New York Times*, June 19, 2013, http://www.nytimes.com/2013/06/20/business/in-head-hunting-big-data-may-not-be-such-a-big-deal.html.

18. Wesley, "Journal," *Works*, vol. 3, 85.

19. W. Edwards Deming, "Large List of Quotes by W. Edwards Deming," *The W. Edwards Deming Institute* (blog), accessed January 8, 2016, http://blog.deming.org/w-edwards-deming-quotes/large-list-of- quotes-by-w-edwards-deming/.

20. Jim Collins, *Good to Great: Why Some Companies Make the Leap . . . and Others Don't* (New York: HarperCollins, 2001), 14.

21. Wesley, "Journal," *Works*, vol. 3, 479.

22. William Morley Punshon, *Lectures* (London: T. Woolmer, 1882), 327.

CHAPTER 9

1. John Wesley, "Journal," *The Works of John Wesley*, vol. 1, 3rd ed. (Kansas City, MO: Beacon Hill, 1979), 5.

2. Ibid., 13, 18.

3. Ibid., 309.

4. John Wesley, "Journal," *The Works of John Wesley*, vol. 2, 3rd ed. (Kansas City, MO: Beacon Hill, 1979), 58.

5. Ibid., 68.

6. Ibid., 224.

7. John Wesley, "Minutes of Several Conversations," *The Works of John Wesley*, vol. 8, 3rd ed. (Kansas City, MO: Beacon Hill, 1979), 311–313.

8. Wesley, "Journal," *Works*, vol. 2, 230.

9. Wesley, "Minutes of Several Conversations," *Works*, 310.

10. Gaylen K. Bunker, ed., "Age of Sages: The Amazing 6th Century BC," Business All Stars, accessed January 8, 2016, http://www.businessallstars.com/sixth.html.

11. John Wesley, "Journal," *The Works of John Wesley*, vol. 4, 3rd ed. (Kansas City, MO: Beacon Hill, 1979), 299.

12. Ibid., 273.

13. Michael Hyatt, "How Real Leaders Demonstrate Accountability," *Michael Hyatt* (blog), March 22, 2012, http://michaelhyatt.com/leadership-and-accountability.html.

14. Patrick Lencioni, "Online Team Assessment Study Reveals Accountability Crisis on Teams," The Table Group, June 24, 2006, http://www.tablegroup.com/newsroom/news/online-team-assessment-study-reveals-accountability-crisis-on-teams.

15. Patrick Lencioni, "Accountability—A Precursor to Success," *The Table Group* (blog), November 2012, http://www.tablegroup.com/blog/thoughts-from-the-field-issue-13-accountability-a-precursor-to-success.

16. Joseph Grenny, "The Best Teams Hold Themselves Accountable," *Harvard Business Review*, May 30, 2014, https://hbr.org/2014/05/the-best-teams-hold-themselves-accountable/.

17. Wesley, "Journal," *Works*, vol. 2, 224, 231, 290.

18. Wesley, "Journal," *Works*, vol. 4, 213.

19. Ibid., 194.

20. Wesley, "Minutes of Several Conversations," *Works*, 308–309.

21. Wesley, "Journal," *Works*, vol. 2, 222.

22. John Wesley, "Journal," *The Works of John Wesley*, vol. 3, 3rd ed. (Kansas City, MO: Beacon Hill, 1979), 423.

23. Wesley, "Minutes of Several Conversations," *Works*, 310.

CHAPTER 10

1. David J. Bosch, *Transforming Mission: Paradigm Shifts in Theology of Mission*, 20th ann. ed., American Society of Missiology Series, no. 16 (Maryknoll, NY: Orbis, 2011), 539.

2. John Wesley, "Minutes of Several Conversations," *The Works of John Wesley*, vol. 8, 3rd ed. (Kansas City, MO: Beacon Hill, 1979), 300.

3. John Wesley, "Introductory Letter," *The Works of John Wesley*, vol. 1, 3rd ed. (Kansas City, MO: Beacon Hill, 1979), 9–10.

4. John Wesley, "An Earnest Appeal to Men of Reason and Religion," *The Works of John Wesley*, vol. 8, 3rd ed. (Kansas City, MO: Beacon Hill, 1979), 8.

5. John Wesley, "A Farther Appeal to Men of Reason and Religion," *The Works of John Wesley*, vol. 8, 3rd ed. (Kansas City, MO: Beacon Hill, 1979), 113.

6. Ibid., 230–231.

7. Ibid., 231.

8. Ibid., 224–225.

9. Ibid., 239.

10. Wesley, "Minutes of Several Conversations," *Works*, 313.

11. Ibid., 310.

12. Ibid., 312.
13. John Wesley, "A Plain Account of the People Called Methodists," *The Works of John Wesley*, vol. 8, 3rd ed. (Kansas City, MO: Beacon Hill, 1979), 254.
14. Ibid.
15. Nick Craig and Scott A. Snook, "From Purpose to Impact," *Harvard Business Review*, May 2014, https://hbr.org/2014/05/from-purpose-to-impact.
16. Retrieved from my notes and correspondence from Dr. Laurel Buckingham. For more information, contact Dr. Buckingham at the Buckingham Leadership Institute: www.kingswood.edu/bli.
17. Wesley, "Minutes of Several Conversations," *Works*, 304.
18. Ibid., 333.
19. John Wesley, "Letters to His Brother Charles," *The Works of John Wesley*, vol. 12, 3rd ed. (Kansas City, MO: Beacon Hill, 1979), 138–139.

CONCLUSION

1. John Wesley, "Repentance of Believers," *The Works of John Wesley*, vol. 5, 3rd ed. (Kansas City, MO: Beacon Hill, 1979), 161.
2. Emil Brunner, *The Word and the World* (London: SCM Press, 1931), 108.
3. John Wesley, "Thoughts upon Methodism," *The Works of John Wesley*, vol. 13, 3rd ed. (Kansas City, MO: Beacon Hill, 1979), 258, 260–261.
4. John Wesley, "A Farther Appeal to Men of Reason and Religion," *The Works of John Wesley*, vol. 8, 3rd ed. (Kansas City, MO: Beacon Hill, 1979), 198.
5. John Wesley, "Journal," *The Works of John Wesley*, vol. 4, 3rd ed. (Kansas City, MO: Beacon Hill, 1979), 341.
6. Ibid., 238.
7. John Wesley, "Journal," *The Works of John Wesley*, vol. 3, 3rd ed. (Kansas City, MO: Beacon Hill, 1979), 295.

APPENDIX A

1. John Wesley, "Minutes of Several Conversations," *The Works of John Wesley*, vol. 8, 3rd ed. (Kansas City, MO: Beacon Hill, 1979), 309–310.

APPENDIX B

1. John Wesley, "Advice to the People Called Methodists," *The Works of John Wesley*, vol. 8, 3rd ed. (Kansas City, MO: Beacon Hill, 1979), 352–353.